ABBA

The Scrapbook

Jean-Marie Potiez

Plexus, London

I dedicate this book to my friend, my 'brother' and my ABBA companion Philippe Elan.

All rights reserved including the right
of reproduction in whole or in part in any form
Copyright © 2009 by Jean-Marie Potiez
This edition copyright © 2009 by Plexus Publishing Limited
Published by Plexus Publishing Limited
25 Mallinson Road
London SW11 1BW
First printing 2009
www.plexusbooks.com

British Library Cataloguing in Publication Data

Potiez, Jean-Marie
ABBA : the scrapbook
1. ABBA (Musical group) 2. Singers - Sweden - Biography
3. Rock musicians - Sweden - Biography
I. Title
782.4'2166'0922

ISBN-13: 978-0-85965-422-7
ISBN-10: 0-85965-422-2

Cover and book design by Jean-Marie Potiez
http://abbathescrapbook.online.fr
Printed by Scotprint

By the same author
Abba: The Book; *Abba: La Legende*; *A Tribute to Frida*

The right of Jean-Marie Potiez to be identified as author of
this work has been asserted by him in accordance with
the Copyright, Designs and Patents Act, 1988

CONTENTS

6 AGNETHA

10 BJÖRN

14 BENNY

18 ANNI-FRID

22 1970

30 1971

38 1972

46 1973

54 1974

74 ABBA GLAM

80 1974-75 TOUR

86 1975

108 VIGGSÖ

110 1976

132 1977 TOUR

142 1977

152 ABBA-THE MOVIE

160 1978

174 1979

188 1979 TOUR

198 1980

208 1981

216 1982

224 ABBA & THE CITY

230 AFTER ABBA

Since writing ABBA: The Book, I have wanted to create the most beautiful book published on ABBA, to pay homage to Anni-Frid, Björn, Benny and Agnetha and to thank them in my own way for all the pleasure they have given me since 6 April 1974. It is true to say that they actually changed my life! Even though they separated in 1982, the magic of ABBA lives on and their songs have the same emotional impact on me.

If since the 70s they have made the whole planet sing and dance, it is not by chance but because their music and good humour have put colour into our often grey and aggressive world. The cinema has paid them homage, their songs are sung by numerous artists and a new generation has fallen under the spell of ABBA. So allow me, through this book, to thank them in the best way I can and to share with you my passion and enthusiasm for the ABBA years!

I have put together ABBA: The Scrapbook with all my heart and energies and I wanted this new book to be a visual celebration that would take us back to the mid-70s when ABBA were performing and travelling the world with their magical music. I hope that ABBA: The Scrapbook will make you live (or relive) those wonderful times!

Thank you ABBA and thank you readers!

Jean-Marie Potiez
Paris, October 2008.

At the age of sixteen, Agnetha made her début as a vocalist with a local dance band from Huskvarna called Bernt Enghardt's Orchestra. It was during this time that she broke up with her boyfriend Björn Lilja, which inspired her to write 'Jag Var Så Kär' (I Was So In Love), a song that would soon catapult her to fame. A demo version was recorded and sent to the CBS-Cupol record producer Karl-Gerhard Lundkvist, who was very impressed by Agnetha's voice. A contract was signed and Agnetha recorded four songs at the Philips Studio in Stockholm on 16 October 1967. One month later, the single 'Fölm Med Mig/Jag Var Så Kär' was released. It stormed into the Swedish *Svensktoppen* chart at No. 3 on 28 January 1968. A star was born.

AGNETHA

Agnetha and her boyfriend Björn Lilja, who inspired the song 'Jag Var Så Kär'.

'I had a green dress with polka dots and boots when we went to Cupol. Sven-Olof Walldoff was the arranger and we recorded four songs in one day. They took pictures for the covers the same day too. I was posing; it felt really strange.'

Agnetha was engaged for a year to the young producer Dieter Zimmerman. She recorded eight singles in German between 1968 and 1972 but never made a breakthrough in Germany.

Highest chart positions in the Svensktoppen

Agnetha FÄLTSKOG

3	Jag Var Så Kär..
8	Utan Dej...
9	Den Jag Väntat På..
2	Allting Har Förändrat Sig...................................
9	Nånting Händer Mej..
	*med **Jörgen Edman***
4	Fram För Svenska Sommaren...............................
5	Zigenarvän...

'As long as I can remember, I've had a need to write my own songs. I still think the melodies are OK, but many of the rhymes are terrible. I try to excuse myself by saying I was so young.'

AGNETHA FÄLTSKOG

Cupol

AGNETHA AND BJÖRN — THE POP ROMANCE OF THE YEAR!

Björn with his mother Aina.

Björn (from Västervik), Gunilla Höjer and Lars Wallman (from Norrköping) during a talent contest organised by Sveriges Radio in 1963.

Björn with Stig Anderson in 1969.

'I was in the army for about a year — it should have been eighteen months but I managed to get out early — but I was still doing some gigs with the Hootenanny Singers.' BJÖRN

(finalister i Sveriges Radio-TV:s "Plats på scen")

Jag vänta...
Ann-Ma...
Inge...

GRÖNA LUND

DAGEN H-EXTRA

HOOTENANNY SINGERS på Stora scenen kl. 17 och 21.30! ★ ALICE BABS med ARNE DOMNERUS ORKESTER på Stora scenen kl. 20!

HOOTENANNY SINGERS

This sensational Swedish song group consists of four young men from Västervik, a small town in eastern Sweden. They were discovered in a nationwide talent hunt by the Swedish Broadcasting Corporation in the autumn of 1963.

They quickly caught on with Swedish radio listeners and the record-buying public and were put under contract by Polar Music AB in Stockholm. Bengt Bernhag and Stig Anderson, Polar's producers, who had previously discovered such local artists as The Spotnicks and brought them to fame, became interested in them.

Today, the Hootenanny Singers are a big name not only in Sweden, but all over Scandinavia. Their records have been on the bestseller lists ever since the first one appeared in January 1964. They are more and more sought after for television and radio appearances in Sweden, Norway, Denmark and Finland. No doubt, soon they will have conquered all of Europe.

(POLAR MUSIC press file — 1965)

HOOTENANNY SINGERS FAN CLUB

Om Du vill bli medlem i deras fan-club så kan du skriva till:

HOOTENANNY SINGERS FAN-CLUB
c/o Ann-Christin Lundström
Stadshotellet
Vimmerby (Sverige)

'I got my first guitar when I was eleven, and at grammar school I had decided to get an education as a Master of Engineering. This changed rapidly when we got our first hit with the Hootenanny Singers. It became fun to be an idol.'

HOOT

'Benny and I had the same musical tastes. When he started speaking, our ideas were so similar that it was like I was listening to myself.'

Björn Ulvaeus

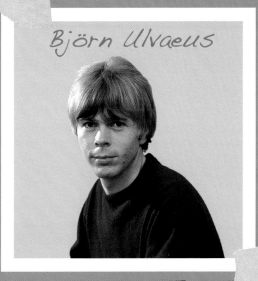

Hansi Schwarz

Tony Rooth

Johan Karlberg

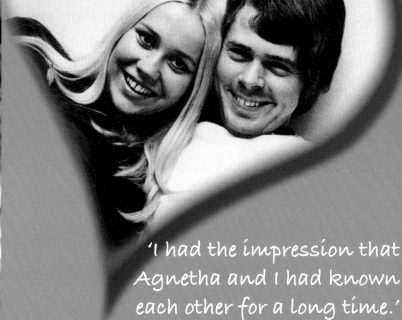

'I had the impression that Agnetha and I had known each other for a long time.'

'Lennart Hegland remembered me from an amateur contest in Bromma, so when the Hep Stars' piano player had to leave the group he called me and asked if I wanted to play with them. After that night I was a member of the Hep Stars.'

In 1964, Benny joined Sweden's nearest equivalent to the Beatles, the Hep Stars. He grew his hair long and became a teen idol alongside the band's singer, Svenne Hedlund.

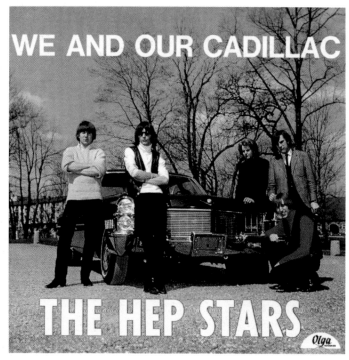

WE AND OUR CADILLAC

THE HEP STARS

Olga

'I wrote "Sunny Girl" at a hotel in Kongsvinger in Norway while Hep Stars were touring. I like the melody but the lyrics still make me embarrassed. I didn't know that much English so I had to write it with a dictionary in my hand.'

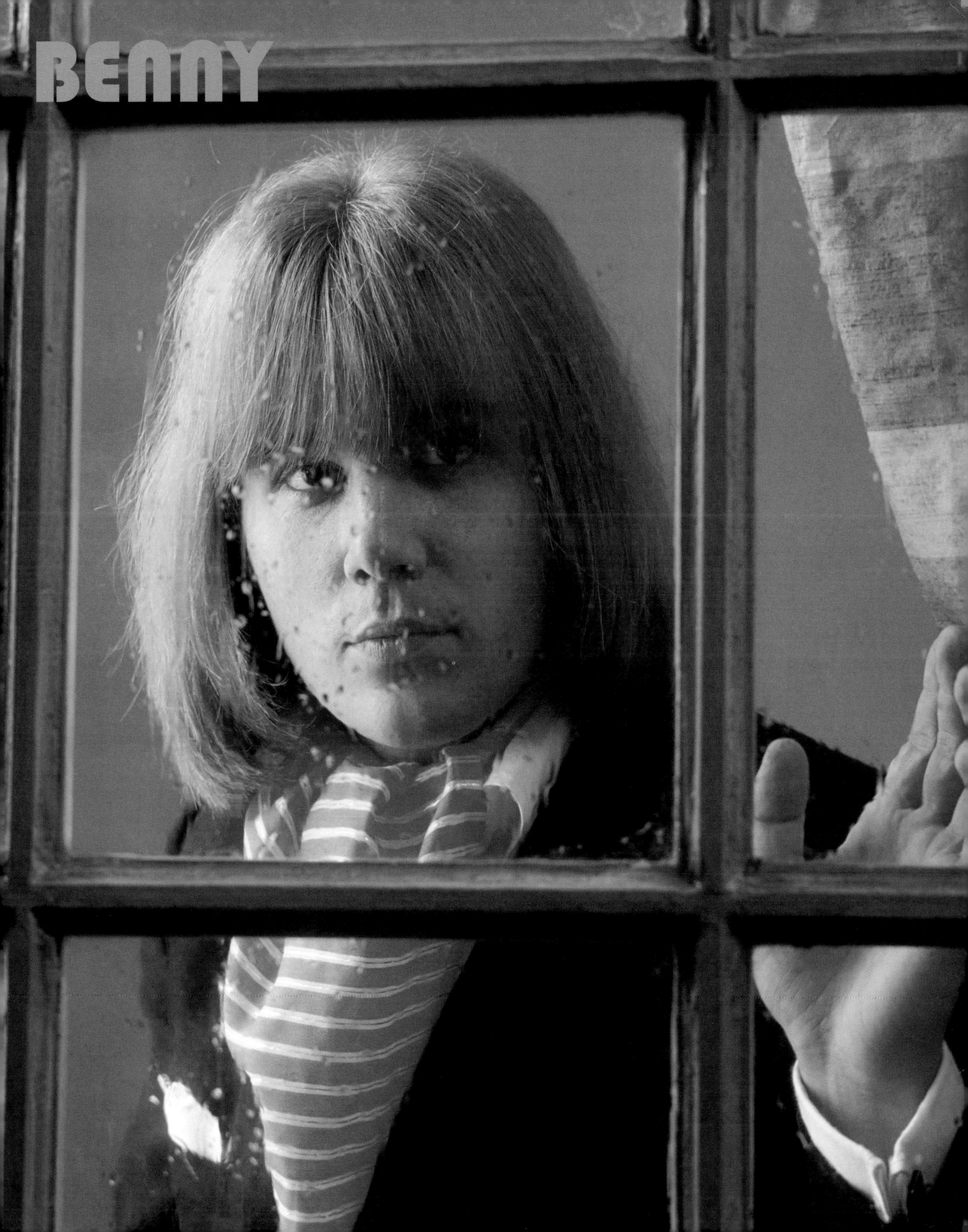
BENNY

THE HEP STARS

THE **HEP STARS**

Christer Pettersson

Svenne Hedlund

Benny Andersson

Janne Frisck

Lennart Hegland

HEP STARS ON STAGE

THE **HEP STARS**

SONGS WE SANG 68

HEP STARS

Highest chart positions in the Svensktoppen

HEP STARS

1	I Natt Jag Drömde Något Som.	
1	Mot Okänt Land	....
4	Sagan Om Lilla Sofi	....
7	Det Finns En Stad	....
7	Tända På Varann	....
4	Speleman	....
3	Är Det Inte Kärlek, Säg	....

DET FINNS EN STAD
T OCH MUSIK: LARS BERGHAGEN
HEP STARS

Lars (Lasse) Berghagen and Benny wrote a number of songs together. Among them were 'It's Been A Long Long Time' and 'Det Finns En Stad'.

'When I write a song it starts with me getting a melody in my head. If I forget about it, it means that it wasn't any good. If I do remember it, I write English lyrics to it. I haven't dared to write Swedish lyrics yet.'

HEP STARS

February 1967 — during the filming of the *Habari-Safari* film in Africa.

ANNI-FRID

3 September 1967 — Anni-Frid won the *Nya Ansikten* national song contest in Stockholm with 'En Ledig Dag'. On the same day, she made her television début on the very popular *Hylands Hörna* programme.
She immediately captivated the viewers with her magical voice and her grace. The following day she signed a contract with EMI Sweden and had her first single released a few weeks later.

'At the time, I was probably more into singers like Ella Fitzgerald and Peggy Lee. Benny was very important when it came to moulding my musical conceptions along more contemporary lines.'

ANNI-FRID
LYNGSTAD
En ledig dag
Peter, kom tillbaka

Din
ANNI-FRID
LYNGSTAD
Du är så underbart rar

ANNI-FRID
LYNGSTAD
Simsalabim
Vi möts igen

ANNI-FRID
LYNGSTAD
MYCKET KÄR • NÄR DU BLIR MIN

Anni-Frid
Lyngstad
Så synd du måste gå
Försök och sov på saken

Anni-Frid
Lyngstad
PETER PAN ★ DU BETONAR KÄRLEK LITE FEL

1 March 1969 — Anni-Frid took part in the *Melodifestivalen*. Her song 'Härlig Är Vår Jord' was well-received by the audience but she finished in joint fourth position with singer Ann-Louise Hanson.

BÖRSENS CABARET

• Charlie Norman Show
med
Anni-Frid Lyngstad
och
Hasse Burman
Dans till
SWEDE 6
Damspecial 5:—

Biljetter till valborgsmäss
afton hos hovmästarna

HAMBURGER BÖRS
Jakobsgat. 6 Tel. 20 49 07, 11 6

Hamburger Börs

PREMIÄR !

S"PREMIÄR
ikväll kl. 22.30

CHARLIE NORM
SHOW
med
nni-Frid Lyngstad
h Hasse Burman
Dans till
nd Millers orkester
 med Siv Gunsnér
ecial Räkcocktail 5:—
burg

BERNS

Charlie Norman • Tjac
Hasse Burman
Laila Dahlin • Annifrid Lyngstad • Mona Thelr
Karl-Axel Källner • Lennie Norman • Sölve Olof
Peter Himmelstrand, Charlie Norman
rzon & Tjadden
Gordon Marsh

In January 1969, Anni-Frid received an offer to work in a cabaret show with veteran pianist and entertainer Charlie Norman, with whom she would work regularly for the following eighteen months. Although she earned good reviews from the critics, none of her first singles was a complete success, as Anni-Frid was probably too jazz orientated for the Swedish charts.

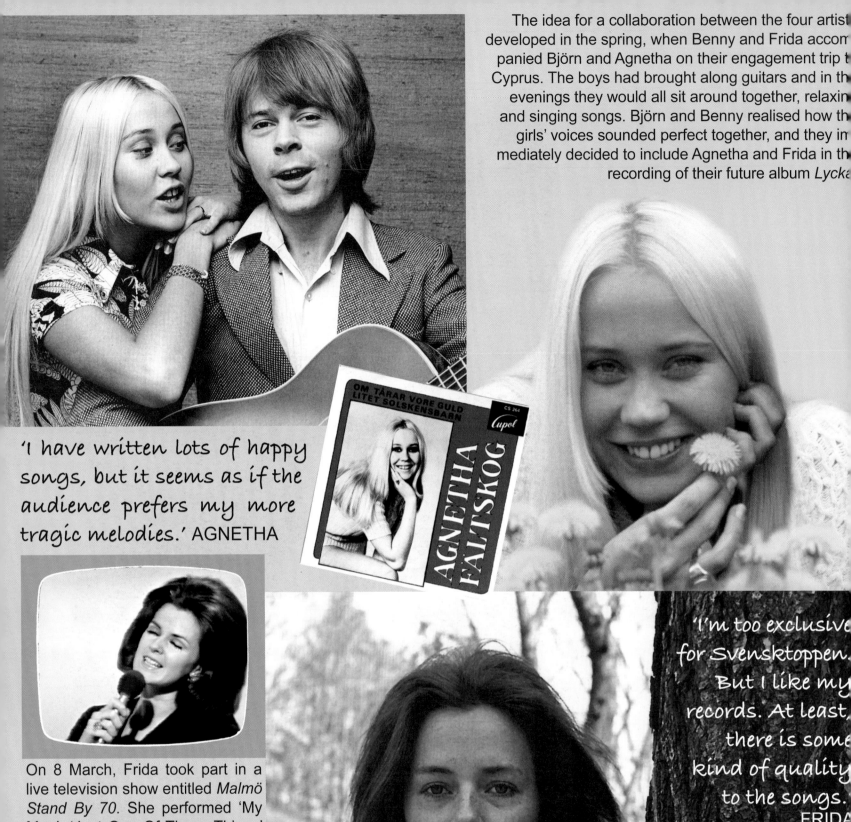

The idea for a collaboration between the four artist developed in the spring, when Benny and Frida accompanied Björn and Agnetha on their engagement trip to Cyprus. The boys had brought along guitars and in the evenings they would all sit around together, relaxing and singing songs. Björn and Benny realised how the girls' voices sounded perfect together, and they immediately decided to include Agnetha and Frida in the recording of their future album *Lycka*.

'I have written lots of happy songs, but it seems as if the audience prefers my more tragic melodies.' AGNETHA

'I'm too exclusive for Svensktoppen. But I like my records. At least, there is some kind of quality to the songs.' FRIDA

On 8 March, Frida took part in a live television show entitled *Malmö Stand By 70*. She performed 'My Man', 'Just One Of Those Things' and 'Mad About The Boy'.

1970

Agnetha Fältskog 'nice girl' (Aftonbladet).

During Summer 1970, Agnetha made a successful tour of Sweden. She was accompanied on stage by singer-comedian Bert-Åke Varg and Rolf Carvenius's orchestra.

Agnetha with Bert-Åke Varg (left) and Rolf Carvenius (right)

Nora

SHOW premiär

Agnetha backstage with Björn, Aina (Björn's mother) and Eva (Björn's sister).

On 7 July, Björn joined his friends Tony Rooth and Hansi Schwarz (from the Hootenanny Singers) for a single concert given as part of the Västervik Song Festival, held in the ruins of Stegeholm Castle. Agnetha went along to support him.

Anni-Frid participated in Swedish Television series *När Stenkakan Slog* (*Remember The Good Old 78s*), which was broadcast in the autumn. The idea of the series was to let contemporary popular singers sing *schlagers* from 1915 to 1955. Anni-Frid performed no less than seven songs.

Anni-Frid with Sten Nilsson.

'At that time, you had to have several hit singles to your credit before you were able to record an entire album. That wasn't the case for me. In addition, my record company considered that I still hadn't found my style. They categorised me too much as a jazz singer and thought that I wasn't commercial enough. Benny let me tackle a repertoire which was more pop-based.' FRIDA

In September, Benny began producing Frida's first album at EMI Studios. She finally seemed to be moving closer towards pop territory: her asso-ciation with him started to open her ears to a form of music she had previously ignored.

frisyr
hårspecialisten

Agnetha, Björn, Benny and Frida posing together for the first time.
The photo session took place on the island of Djurgården in Stockholm.

Haircare products advertising, featuring Benny and Frida.

Björn co-produced Agnetha's new
album and performed a duet with
her entitled 'Så Här Börjar Kärlek'.

Agnetha Fältskog

Som jag är

'Agnetha Fältskog
is not that particular about what
she records, and it showed with the deplora-
ble "Zigenarvän". Her new LP *Som Jag Är* (Cupol)
gives us no reason to reassess that statement. She
sings quite well, but sentimentality lies in wait a bit
too often. The record is nicely arranged by Sven-Olof
Walldoff. However, the material demonstrates that the
day she dares to abandon short cuts to the most com-
mon public taste and cheap success, she will become
someone to count on. But not before then.'
Göran Sellgren (*Expressen*)

"Lycka"/Björn Ulvaeus & Benny Andersson

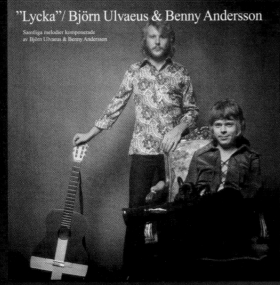

"Lycka"/ Björn Ulvaeus & Benny Andersson

Samtliga melodier komponerade
av Björn Ulvaeus & Benny Andersson

'Hej Gamle Man' was performed on the television programme *I Stället För Tarzan*.

The album *Lycka* contained the very first song to feature all four future ABBA members: 'Hej Gamle Man'. Released as a single B-side, the song became a big hit in Sweden, topping the charts for five consecutive weeks.

'I don't think "Hej Gamle Man" would have become such a hit if Agnetha and I hadn't been on it.'
FRIDA

Björn and Benny with singer/actres Eva Bysing before the television sho *I Stället För Tarzan*.

'The four of us did this horrible cabaret stuff with sketches and monologues and trying to be funny. We also did a little chunk of our own stuff. It gave us the feeling that we should try to make a pop record in English.' BENNY

'The two engaged couples are really cute and that's how they want to be seen.' Viveca Sundvall (Aftonbladet)

In July 1971, the death of Stig Anderson's partner in Polar Music, the record producer Bengt Bernhag led to Benny and Björn's subsequent employment as house producers at the record company.

Björn and Benny concentrated on songwriting: while Benny was putting the finishing touches to Frida's début album, Björn started the production of Agnetha's fourth LP *När En Vacker Tanke Blir En Sång*.

'The competition in thi profession is incredibl hard, only the stronges and best survive. Despi the fact that I love bein an artist... I'm no sure that I'm amon those who wi survive FRID

ANNI-FRID LYNGSTAD

EN LITEN SÅNG OM KÄRLEK
TRE KVART FRÅN NU

EMI
Columbia
4 E006-34313

1971 ÄR "FRIDAS" ÅR

(1971 is Frida's year

1971

FRIDA

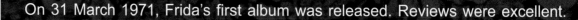

On 31 March 1971, Frida's first album was released. Reviews were excellent.

'The *Frida* album is the perfect exclamation mark. A completely professional product with surprising precision. Not only does she have a voice full of great feeling but she is also sensual and expressive. She sings "Telegram För Fullmånen" so well that she really warms our hearts. It has everything: emotion, warmth and tenderness, which all adds up to make Anni-Frid a rare and intelligent artist.'
Tommy Eriksson *(Folket)*

'It is, in the first place, an LP that is totally professional, from the exceptionally elegant cover to the actual record's innermost, well-arranged track. The material is well chosen and relatively discriminating ... Anni-Frid Lyngstad simply sings unusually intelligently.'
(Dagens Nyheter)

'*Frida* contains almost exclusively slow, slightly romantic songs that actually are rather alike, but which nevertheless do not become monotonous thanks to Anni-Frid's fascinating style of singing.' *(Ystads Allehanda)*

'Anni-Frid Lyngstad has a very sensual and enjoyable voice, and is a skilled, experienced singer.'
Lo Rindberg *(Östersunds Posten)*

'Anni-Frid sings suggestively and seems to have a feeling for most things ... Good tunes, good lyrics, a good artist — a good LP.'
Tony Kaplan *(Arbetet)*

Sida 1

1. **TRE KVART FRÅN NU**   3.14
(A. Rubinstein — Bearb. och text: Peter Himmelstrand)
Musikfabriken

2. **JAG BLIR GALEN NÄR JAG TÄNKER PÅ DEJ**   3.27
(Randazzot — Weinstein — Stig Anderson)
United Artists

3. **LYCKA**   2.59
(Björn Ulvaeus — Benny Andersson — Stig Anderson)
Union Songs AB

4. **SEN DESS HAR JAG INTE SETT 'EN**   2.08
(Trad.arr.: Claes Rosendahl — Lars Berghagen)
Union Songs AB

5. **EN TON AV TYSTNAD**   4.00
(Paul Simon — Owe Junsjö)
Intreco AB

6. **SUZANNE**   3.07
(Leonard Cohen — Owe Junsjö)
Imudico AB

Arr. och dir.: Claes Rosendahl (1, 3, 4 och 6), Bengt Palmers (2 och 5)

Sida 2

1. a) **ALLTING SKALL BLI BRA**

   b) **VAD GÖR JAG MED MIN KÄRLEK**   6.14
(Rice—Webber—Peter Himmelstrand)
Universalfilm AB

2. **JAG ÄR BEREDD**   2.38
(Paul Leka—Denise Gross—Stig Anderson)
United Artists

3. **EN LITEN SÅNG OM KÄRLEK**   2.25
(S. Fine—Lars Berghagen)
Chappell Nordiska AB

4. **TELEGRAM FÖR FULLMÅNEN**   1.59
(Cornelis Vreeswijk)
Multitone

5. **BARNEN SOVER**   3.35
(Peter Himmelstrand)
Musikfabriken

'Min Egen Stad' went straight into the *Svensktoppen* at No. 3. The song, which stayed in the charts for seven weeks, reached No. 1 on 7 November. It was the first real hit for the singer, and prompted EMI to issue a new pressing of the *Frida* album, featuring the hit single.

E 062-34360

STEREO

Rak och enkel underhållning
med Björn, Agnetha och Benn

AGNETHA, BJÖRN, BENNY
Parken, Simontorp

Årets Svensktoppspar —
ifter sig om en månad
kligen **Björn Ul-**
ha **Fältskog.**

Och man kan konstatera:
● Agnetha Fältskog har blivit
säkrare och mer scenmedveten
— och dessutom vinnlagt sig att
sjunga rent;
Björn Ulvaeus har dämpat sina

*Årets Svensktoppspar —
Agnetha Fältskog . . .*

*. och Björn Ulvaeus. D
n en månad.*

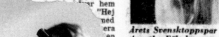

On 30 April, Björn, Benny and Agnetha embarked on a 60-date Folkpark tour. They were accompanied on stage by Göran Lagerberg on bass and Kjell Jeppson on drums. They performed only at weekends and had time for several recording sessions in the interim.

STARLETS IDOLPORTRÄTT
Agneta, Björn, Benny

Midsommardans Från Solliden TV programme.

Björn and Agnetha were married in the little church of Verum, a parish of Skåne in southern Sweden. The couple tried to keep the ceremony secret but more than 3000 people converged on the village to witness the 'wedding of the year'. Björn's best man was Hans 'Berka' Bergkvist, while his sister Eva and Agnetha's sister Mona served as bridesmaids. Frida, on tour with Lasse Berghagen in the north of Sweden, was unable to make the celebrations. The wedding supper was held at Wittsjöhus castle with smoked eel, tournedos and Arctic berry ice-cream on the menu. The party continued late into the night.

'Sunny Girl', the bridal couple's wedding dance, performed by Svenne Hedlund with his wife Lotta on drums and Benny on piano.

The newlyweds with Björn's sister Eva and Hans 'Berka' Bergkvist.

RÖSTER I RADIO-TV — *med hela midsommar-programmet!*

Nr 27 25 juni—2 juli 1971 1:75 inkl. moms

FOTO: ULF STRAHLE

Lasse Berghagen Annifrid Lyngstad **SOL**

Frida och Lasse på sommartoppen

While Agnetha, Björn and Benny toured togethe
Anni-Frid went on the road with Lars Berghager
Before the tour, Lars and Frida had recorded tw
duets which were released as a single: 'En Kvä
Om Sommaren' and 'Vi Vet Allt Men Nästan Inget
The first reached No. 8 in the *Svensktoppen*.

Lars Berghagen and Anni-Frid singing 'Vi Vet Allt Men Nästan Inget' in the television
programme *Vem Har Snott Midsommarkransen?*

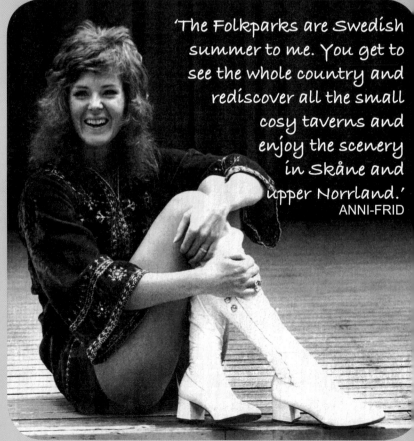

'The Folkparks are Swedish
summer to me. You get to
see the whole country and
rediscover all the small
cosy taverns and
enjoy the scenery
in Skåne and
upper Norrland.'
ANNI-FRID

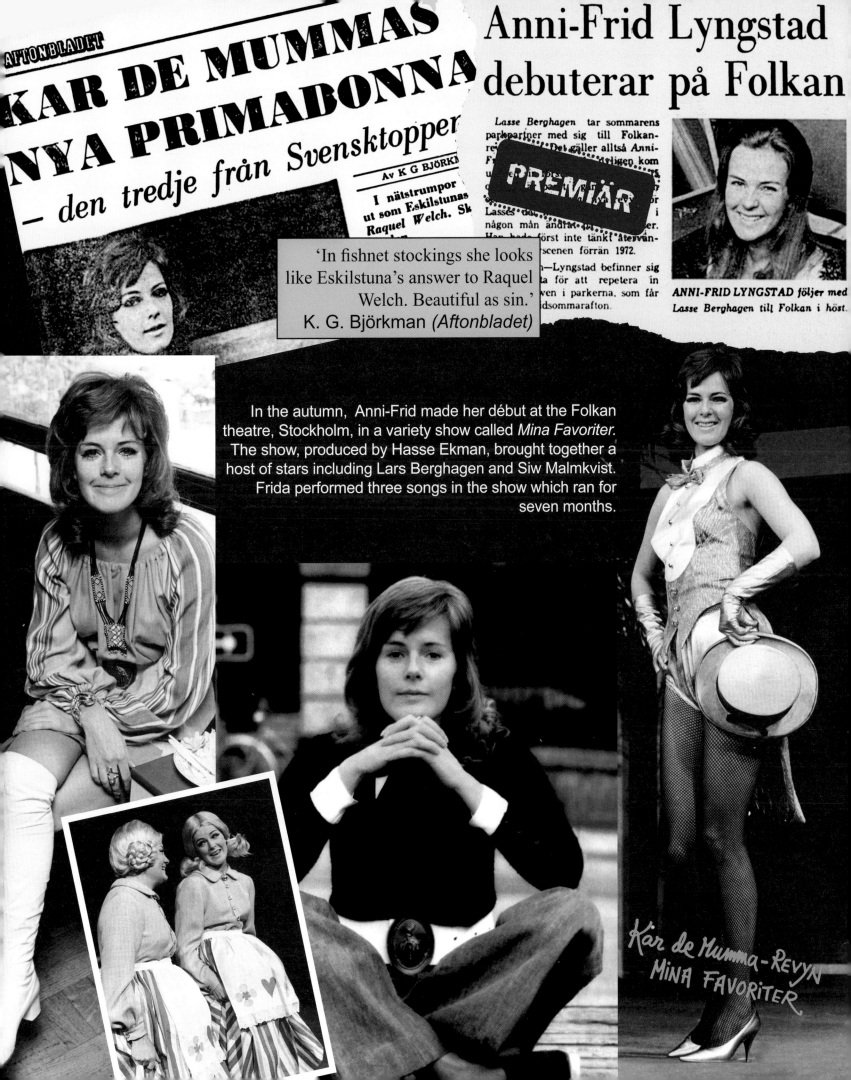

KAR DE MUMMAS NYA PRIMADONNA

— den tredje från Svensktoppen

Av K G BJÖRKM

I nätstrumpor
ut som Eskilstunas
Raquel Welch. Sk

'In fishnet stockings she looks like Eskilstuna's answer to Raquel Welch. Beautiful as sin.'
K. G. Björkman *(Aftonbladet)*

AFTONBLADET

Anni-Frid Lyngstad debuterar på Folkan

Lasse Berghagen tar sommarens
parkpariner med sig till Folkan-
re Det gäller alltså Anni-
F igen kom
u i
Lasses
någon mån ändra er. i
Han hade först inte tänkt återvän
scenen förrän 1972.
—Lyngstad befinner sig
a för att repetera in
en i parkerna, som får
dsommarafton.

PREMIÄR

ANNI-FRID LYNGSTAD *följer med Lasse Berghagen till Folkan i höst.*

In the autumn, Anni-Frid made her début at the Folkan theatre, Stockholm, in a variety show called *Mina Favoriter*. The show, produced by Hasse Ekman, brought together a host of stars including Lars Berghagen and Siw Malmkvist. Frida performed three songs in the show which ran for seven months.

Kar de Mumma-Revyn
MINA FAVORITER

At the start of the year, the two couples moved into brand-new town houses in Vallentuna, one of Stockholm's northernmost suburbs.

Anni-Frid and Benny at home with their dog Zappa.

'Benny, Björn, Agnetha and I spend a lot of time together. Especially since now we are neighbours here in Vallentuna. Before, we didn't know each other that well but we've got to know each other with time.' FRIDA

It was a depressing time for Frida. She was living far from her children, suffering the failure of her last EMI single, and tired of singing at the Folkan Theatre every night. She began to doubt everything and even considered abandoning her musical career — going so far as to register with a fashion college in Stockholm. However, she would soon get back on her feet thanks to new projects she embarked upon with her future ABBA colleagues!

At the end of January, Björn and Benny travelled to London with seventeen-year-old singer Lena Andersson to record the Swedish and English versions of 'Säg Det Med En Sång'. Although a jury of people from the music business voted the song only third at the *Melodivestivalen*, it became a hit in Sweden, reaching No.1 in the *Svensktoppen*.

1972

Den svenska originalutgåvan av Andrew Lloyd Webber's och Tim Rice's rock-opera

JESUS CHRIST SUPERSTAR

PHILIPS

Agnetha played the part of Mary Magdalene in the Swedish version of the Tim Rice/Andrew Lloyd Webber musical *Jesus Christ Superstar*. A single, produced by Björn, was released featuring two songs from the show. After her performances at the Scandinavium in Gothenburg, Agnetha left the company to prepare for her summer tour. Her role was taken over by Titti Sjöblom.

US CHRIST SUPERSTAR
SÅLT 18.19. 20. FEB.
— 25 KL 19.30
— UP FRIIDROTT.

Titti Sjöblom, Agnetha Fältskog and Funny Holmqvist.

Congratulations, Agnetha!

'She's My Kind Of Girl', which had flopped in Sweden in 1970, unexpectedly became a No. 1 smash hit in Japan. Encouraged by this success, Björn and Benny decided to write more pop songs in English. The first track to be recorded was 'People Need Love' and this time the boys decided to let the girls' voices be more prominent. After a long hard day's work, the very first ABBA song was born.

'I remember thinking that "now we have made our first really good record", and I think Björn felt the same way.' BENNY

ÅRET RUNT

Nr 30 17 Juli 1972 PRIS 2:—

Agnetha Fältskog:

JAG SKA BLI MAMMA!

Stor artikelserie:
DE NYA UTVANDRARNA

Skall de rädda Sverige?

A great event was to occur early in the summer: Agnetha was pregnant with her first child. Björn and Agnetha talked to the media about their joy at expecting the baby they had wanted for so long.

Agnetha, Sten Nilsson and Annika Risberg in the TV show *Gammeldans*.

The summer saw Agnetha embark on her tour of the Swedish parks. On stage, she was joined by the four dancers from the Cocco ballet.

People need love

BJÖRN & BENNY with **FRIEDA & ANNA**
MERRY·GO·ROUND (En Karusell)

'We wanted to try something new, find a new way. So we decided to go for the English market. The really early successes were fantastic.'
FRIDA

'People Need Love', credited to Björn & Benny, Agnetha & Anni-Frid, became a significant hit in Sweden, reaching No. 17 on the charts. The single was even released in a few other countries but it never became a hit outside Scandinavia. The success of 'People Need Love' followed by 'He's Your Brother' encouraged the two couples to record an album as a group.

HE IS YOUR BROTHER

Musik & text: Benny Andersson, Björn Ulvaeus
Union Songs AB

Inspelad av Björn & Benny, Agnetha & Anni-Frid
på Polar POS 1168

I distribution: Sweden Music AB, Nybrogatan 53, Stockholm

ANNI-FRID LYNGSTAD
MAN VILL JU LEVA LITE DESSEMELLAN
SKA MAN SKRATTA ELLER GRÅTA

POS 1161

While touring Sweden with jazz guitarist and singer Roffe Berg in the autumn, Frida topped the Swedish charts for the second time in her career with the single 'Man Vill Ju Leva Lite Dessemellan'.

43

Christmas in Vallentuna
with
Agnetha, Björn, Benny and
Anni-Frid

From now on, Björn, Benny, Agnetha and Anni-Frid would be working together full-time as a group and Stig intended to ensure that his four protégés would be successful beyond the borders of Scandinavia. When they were invited to write a song for the Swedish selections for the 1973 Eurovision Song Contest, Stig saw it was an unmissable opportunity. The song they came up with was 'Ring Ring'. With the aid of their invaluable sound engineer, Michael B. Tretow, they drew some inspiration from the legendary producer Phil Spector when the track was recorded.

Björn with Lena Andersson in the TV programme Får Vi Lämnar Några Blommor?

Michael B. Tretow

Ring, Ring

Words and Music by
Benny Andersson, Björn Ulvaeus
and Stig Anderson

English lyric by
Neil Sedaka and Phil Cody

bright Rock

1973

On 10 February, the *Melodifestivalen* was held and to everyone's astonishment, the two couples only finished third. They were deeply disappointed but the success of 'Ring Ring' in Sweden as well as outside Scandinavia proved that the Swedish jury of so-called experts had chosen the wrong Eurovision entry for 1973.

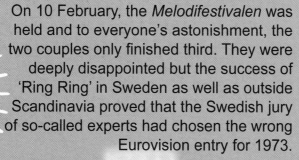

'I was terribly nervous in the hours before the TV show. Just as I was going onto the stage, the baby started kicking. That's why I had to stay in the background, so I could get off the stage quickly if something happened.'
AGNETHA

appy parents: Björn and Agnetha with daughter Linda
in, born on 23 February at Danderyd hospital, Stockholm.

Two days after the *Melodifestivalen*, Frida travelled to Caracas (Venezuela) with Stig and Lena Andersson to represent Sweden in the Onda Nueva song festival.

Stig was eager to promote 'Ring Ring' outside the borders of Scandinavia. The foreign release of the single would be supported
by a promotional tour of several Northern European countries. Agnetha didn't take part in the
trip, as she was looking after the baby. This is Inger
Brundin, one of Anni-Frid's friends, who stood in for
her. Nobody noticed the change as the quartet weren't
sufficiently well-known outside Scandinavia.

TV show *Spotlight* in Austria.

Anni-Frid and Benny with bassist Rutger Gunnarsson.

På turné

Vretstorps FOLKETS PARK
Lördag 21—01
WERNER LUNDS ORK.
Show Kl. 23 Show

Björn Benny Agnetha & Frida

Björn's glittery overall.

The two couples toured the Swedish parks from 15 June until 9 September. So that the tour wouldn't interfere with their studio work or Björn and Agnetha's family life, the group chose to perform only at weekends. Accompanied by three musicians (bassist Rutger Gunnarsson, drummer Kjell Jeppson and Hans 'Berka' Bergkvist), Agnetha, Björn, Benny and Frida gave their audiences a 30-minute show.

Benny and Frida posing (in 1974) in their 1973 glittery stage outfits.

'We travelled a lot and did a lot of television in Northern Europe for "Ring Ring". That was quite good for us. We were prepared for what was going to come.' BJÖRN

20 June — Tivoli amusement park in Copenhagen (Denmark).

The four Swedes with Norwegian producer Knut Lie.

At the beginning of August, the two couples went to Oslo to perform 'Ring Ring' on the TV show *Momarkedet*. All the profits from this famous Norwegian programme went to the Red Cross.

On 13 August, Stig celebrated the tenth anniversary of the record company Polar Music as well as the tenth anniversary of the Hootenanny Singers. He took the opportunity of that big night to present awards to the artists on the label.

Photo: Björn, Benny, Hansi Schwarz, Ted Gärdestad and Tony Rooth behind Agnetha, Stig and Anni-Frid.

The hectic schedule and the pressure of the media confirmed that there was a future in the group concept. Shortly after the two couples had completed their summer tour, they began work on their next album. With about half the LP completed, it was announced that Benny, Björn and Stig had indeed been invited to submit a song for the 1974 Swedish Eurovision selection. It was also decided to change their unmanageable name into a group name easy to pronounce abroad. 'ABBA', the combination of the initials of the members' first names, was adopted after permission had been granted by Abba, the Swedish canned fish company.

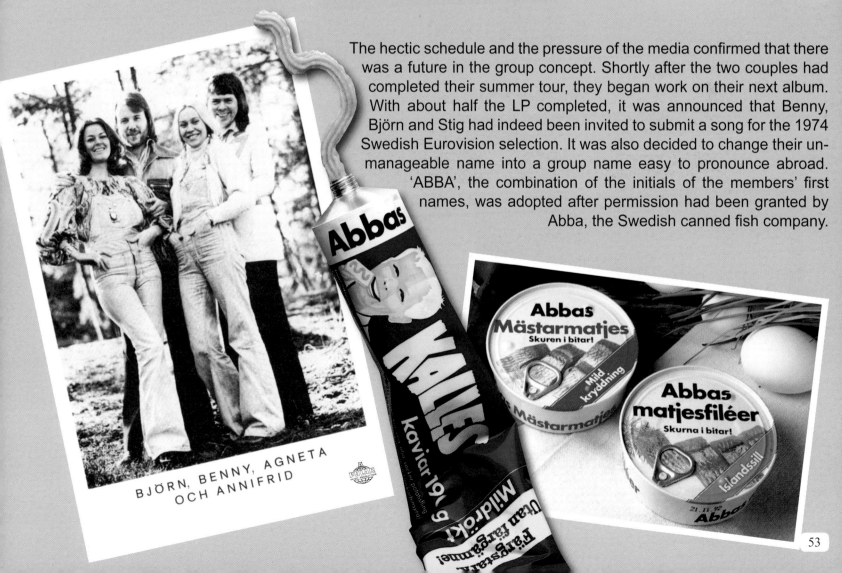

BJÖRN, BENNY, AGNETA OCH ANNIFRID

53

The Melodifestivalen

On 9 February, 'Waterloo' won the *Melodifestivalen* by a knockout. The Swedish People's Jury (165 men and women of all ages) gave it 302 points out of a possible 495. ABBA's performance was excellent and their conductor Sven-Olof Walldoff caused a sensation in his Napoleon costume! The songwriting team of Ulvaeus, Andersson and Anderson had come up with a sound that both jury and audience enjoyed enormously. The evening came to a close with a massive party organised by Stig at his villa in Nacka.

The photographer Ola Lager organised the photo shoot in the magnificent setting of the sixteenth-century Gripsholm Castle, just outside Mariefred, 50 kilometres west of Stockholm. Bassist Mike Watson wore the Napoleon uniform in the photos.

Mike Watson

Making the album sleeve

The original album sleeve was designed by Ron Spaulding (Ola's artistic director in 1974) featuring the Souvenir Light Italic typeface.

ABBA (BJÖRN, BENNY, AGNETHA & FRIDA)

The 'Waterloo' outfits

ANNI-FRID

had a shop on Norrlands-
gatan, in the city centre.
Benny and Frida visited
me from time to time to
buy some clothes. In 1974,
they had decided they'd
win the Melodifestivalen.
They asked me to design
their stage outfits in the
glam-rock style which was
very trendy at that time.
They cost about 100 dollars
each. So cheap compared
to today's costs!'
INGER SVENNEKE

The four costumes
were decorated with
buttons featuring Stan
Laurel, Marlene Dietrich
and the American
silent-film comedian
Harry Langdon.

AGNETHA

Arrival in the United Kingdom.

Opening the telegrams.

By a happy coincidence, the group stayed in the *Napoleon* suite at the Grand Hotel in Brighton. Unfortunately, between rehearsals, interviews, photo sessions and meetings with potential distributors, they had little time to visit the town.

The Music People at
EUROVISION

EUROVISION SONG CONTEST 1974
Name STIG ANDERSON
Function DELEGATE
Country SWEDEN

DOME BRIGHTON

ISION SONG CONTEST

SATURDAY, 6th APRIL, 1974

ROW E 12 STALLS CIRCLE

CHILDREN UNDER 14 NOT ADMITTED

SECURITY ARRANGEMENTS WILL BE IN FORCE
AND WE ASK YOUR KIND CO-OPERATION

NO SMOKING PERMITTED IN THE AUDITORIUM

NOT TRANSFERABLE

EUROVISION
CONTEST

DOORS O

NO A
AFT

STAGE DOOR

'No one can imagine the tension of such an event. Your skin crawls, your stomach knots up and your throat gets all dry. You want to run away from it all.' BJÖRN

La première chance du groupe ABBA s'appelle « Waterloo »

1er GRAND PRIX EUROVISION 1974

Seger med Waterloo

Stig rushed onstage to accept his songwriting award and proceeded to repeat the phrase 'thank you' in several languages.

After the contest, the celebrations in Brighton continued. The group didn't get to bed until 6am the following morning.

Abba-dabba-doo — it's Euro's Waterloo

LONDON

During their stay in London, the two couples tried to give themselves some time to do a little shopping, despite their hectic timetable of press conferences, radio interviews, photo sessions in Hyde Park and at Waterloo station. They also performed on Britain's most popular TV pop-music programme, *Top Of The Pops*.

Reception with the Swedish ambassador to Britain, Ole Jödahl.

NY LP

WATERLOO   ABBA (BJÖRN, BENNY, AGNETHA & FRIDA)

POLAR POLS 252

WATERLOO   ABBA (BJÖRN, BENNY, AGNETHA & FRIDA)

The *Waterloo* album features a lot of great singing by Agnetha and Frida, alone, in unison and singing along wih Björn. It also contains 'Suzy-Hang-Around': the only ABBA song to feature Benny on lead vocals.

'Strictly speaking it is of course completely meaningless to "give one's opinion" about this album. The Swedish people have voted for ABBA and "Waterloo" and that's that . . . Obviously the record will become a so-called monster seller. Moreover, it is practically computer programmed, skilfully handcrafted and – of course – in English. Björn and Benny have skimmed the surface, or rather the surfaces, of our current pop trends. Together they also remember how they used to sound:
– "Honey Honey" and "Suzy-Hang-Around" resemble early Beach Boys (although ABBA do not sing as well, of course);
– "Watch Out" is a tentative soul effort – where Agnetha and Anni-Frid, who otherwise do a decent job, for self-evident reasons fall short;
– "Gonna Sing You My Lovesong" is a "blue" ballad similar to Leon Russell's gospel style;
– "Sitting In The Palmtree" is West Indies-influenced reggae pop;
– "Hasta Manana" has characteristics of German schlager . . .

Accordingly, one cannot complain about the variety. And everybody who has previously thought ABBA too tame gets plenty of songs with a bang, as well as Janne Schaffer's guitar. However, it is not clear where Björn and Benny themselves stand in this mixture of styles. They are obviously clever. But for my own part, I would rather see a musician's personality than this show of versatility. And hear a bit less of the moog and mellotron, with which Benny Andersson replaces all the background music.'

Hans Fridlund *(Expressen)*

ABBA 1974 SUMMER TOUR

CANCELLED

JUNE			
Friday	21	Trehörningsjö	
Saturday	22	Hede	
Sunday	23	Kongsberg (Norway)	
Wednesday	26	Eskilstuna	23.00
Friday	28	Gävle	
Saturday	29	Östervål	

			22.00

JULY			22.30
Friday	5	Björneborg	
Saturday	6	Borlänge	
Wednesday	10	Bjurberget	
Friday	12	Skellefteå	
Saturday	13	Mohed	22.00
Sunday	14	Hammerdal	22.00
Wednesday	17	Kristianopel	23.00
Thursday	18	Simonstorp	22.00
Friday	19	Mjölby	21.00
Saturday	20	Växjö	
Sunday	21	Malmö	22.30
Thursday	25	Stockholm	01.00
Friday	26	Köping	22.00
Saturday	27	Gamleby	
Sunday	28	Visby	

(Unfinished calendar of the cancelled tour)

Following their victory in Brighton, ABBA got an enormous number of offers from several countries including the United States. Stig and the group then decided to cancel the tour of the Swedish public parks, which had previously been verbally agreed with the promoters, to concentrate on their foreign promotional activities. A difficult decision which was violently criticised by the Folkpark organisations and the Swedish newspapers.

'Winning the Eurovision Song Contest was a lot of fun, but after that came a period of work which was so intense that it was difficult to enjoy the success.' AGNETHA

Die Aktuelle Schaubude.

GERMANY

ABBA performing 'Waterloo' in German on NDR/N3 channel.

TV show *Domino*.

RTL Non Stop radio programme.

FRANCE

Waterloo

ABBA
ANNIFRID · BENNY · BJORN · ANNA
Conquering Europe!

...ds and Mus...
...ersson, Bjö...
...Stig Ander...

The Eddy Becker Show.

ABBA

THE NETHERLANDS

DENMARK

TV show *Toppop*.

69

Kings and Queens of the charts!

2 HONEY, HONEY ABBA

3 MY TEENAGE QUEEN Harpo

4 EVERYDAY Slade
5 I SEE A STAR Mouth & McNeal
6 TEENAGE RAMPAGE Sweet
7 SEASONS IN THE SUN Terry Jacks
8 WATERLOO ABBA
9 THE LOCOMOTION Grand Funk

10 HASTA MANANA ABBA
11 DINGA LINGA LENA Pugh
12 KING KONG SONG ABBA
13 MONKEY SONG Douglas
14 THE ENTERTAINER Marvin Hamlish
15 THE SHOW MUST GO ON Leo Sayer

16 BILLY DON'T BE A HERO Paper Lace
17 BOLLA OCH RULLA Pugh
18 ROLL AWAY THE STONE Mott The Hoople
19 BURN Deep Purple
20 DEVIL GATE DRIVE Suzie Quatro
21 MAMA STRIKES BACK Small & Tall

TIFFANYS TOP TWENTY

Top Of The Pops — December.

UNITED KINGDOM

Top Of The Pops — 30 April.

'So Long' on *Kid Jensen's 45* TV programme.

ANNIFRID BENNY BJORN ANNA

ABBA
Conquering Europe!

Chansons à la Carte.

After Brussels, ABBA made a brief stop to Waterloo where the mayor had arranged for them to visit his town.

Summer break on the island of Viggsö.

ABBA............honey honey

ABBA
in the
★★★★★★★ UNITED STATES

ABBA with the Swedish Consul to New York, Gunnar Lonaeus.

Ein Kessel Buntes TV show — East Germany.

ABBA's return to Swedish television in the programme *Nygammalt.*

1973, 1974 and 1975 were the glam years for ABBA. Their look and their sound were directly inspired by artists like David Bowie, Slade, Sweet and Mud.

'It was the era of glam-rock: Sweet, Gary Glitter. We thought that, to make an impact, we had to look as outrageous as possible. The word "camp" came later!'
BJÖRN

ABBA GLAM

NORA

'Agnetha's overall was all made in stretch material. As far as Frida's costume is concerned, we produced a mini-skirt slit into several strips together with a skintight bolero. Both girls wore satin capes designed like a mini-jacket so they could open them.' OWE SANDSTRÖM

'Our platform shoes were made in London, and every time they had to have bigger heels!' BJÖRN

Rehearsals in the amphitheatre of the Rudbeck school in Sollentuna, 6-15 November 1974

Rehearsals at the Jarla theatre, Stockholm, June 1975

During the winter 1974-1975, ABBA embarked on a tour separated in two sessions. The group played in Germany, Austria, Switzerland and Scandinavia. On stage, they were backed by the Beatmakers and put on a complete glam-rock show with special lighting effects and soap bubbles, which climaxed with a firework display. In June 1975, ABBA were back on the road for a fourteen-date tour of the Swedish parks, where they attracted more than 100,000 spectators.

1974-1975 TOUR

On The Road With ABBA

ABBA PÅ EUROPA-TURNÉ · ABBA PÅ EUROPA-TURNÉ · ABBA PÅ EUROPA-TURNÉ · ABBA PÅ TURNÉ

STOCKHOLMS KONSERTHUS
STORA SALEN

ABBA

Lördag 11 januari 1975 kl. 21.00

1:a Radens Sida   Dörr **III**

VÄNSTER   Bänk **2**

Garderob **C**   Plats **56**

Kr 40:— + Kr 1:— garderob

On The Road With ABB A

Backstage in Stockholm with ABBA fan Anna Lindkvist (73-years-old!).

Gold for ABBA in Oslo.

10 January — Press conference in Oslo before the concert at Chateau Neuf

'So Long' on the *Disco* TV show (Germany).

20 January — Gold for ABBA during the Helsinki concert.

Promotional visit to Paris in the beginning of February.

1975

March — Rehearsing 'SOS' in *Toppop*.

March — 'I Do, I Do, I Do, I Do, I Do' in *Toppop*.

Early April — *The Eddy Go Round Show.*

Björn, Agnetha and Linda off for a week's holiday in Crete.

I do, I do, I do, I do, I do

(Benny Andersson, Stig Anderson & Björn Ulvaeus)

KLUGER INTERNATIONAL

8, rue FERNAND NEURAY straat . 1060 BRUXELLES BRUSSEL

'Rock Me'

In Brussels, the group took part in the programme *Chansons à la Carte*.

Rehearsals.

'I Do, I Do, I Do, I Do, I Do'

TIO I TOPP — SVENSKA LISTAN
ABBA
I do I do I do

'This week's misses: It's too late, kids. Teach-In are the champs now you're not likely to do anything about it with this turgid mess. "I Do, I Do, I Do, I Do, I Do" sounds like Vera Lynn having an argument with Dorothy Squires in the showers. It's so bad it hurts. We can all do without it. A Miss!'
Colin Irwin (*Melody Maker*)

April in Paris on the lake of the Bois de Boulogne.

ABBA

In early 1975, ABBA finished recording and putting the finishing touches to the last songs on their new album, due to be released that spring. The band had a heavy work schedule, with studio sessions being interrupted by promotional tours around Europe for 'So Long' and 'I Do, I Do, I Do, I Do, I Do'. For the album cover, Stig Anderson wanted to work again with Ola Lager who did the photography for the *Waterloo* album. He organised a meeting in March where everyone put their ideas forward. Björn and Benny brought along a tape of the songs. Ola came along with his wife, who often helped out with the style and accessories for her husband's photo sessions, and his artistic director Ron Spaulding. Björn and Benny played the tape to the others, even though some of the songs had not yet been mixed. As often occurs in this kind of meeting, all kinds of ideas were brought up, including the eccentric! As was always the case at Polar Music, they worked and laughed a lot. Frida mentioned the new costumes designed by Owe Sandström, but this time the group didn't want to wear their stage costumes on the album cover. An original and bold idea was needed. Listening to 'Mamma Mia', Ron Spaulding suggested a retro atmosphere. The idea was unanimously agreed, but a style and image still had to be found. Stig and the four members of the group ended the meeting by giving *carte blanche* to Ron, Ola and his wife to come up with the visual concept for the new album. Several days later, a conversation with the designer Rune Söder-

qvist started to move the preparations forward. Rune pointed out to his friend Ola that there was an interesting retro hotel 150 metres from his studio in Riddargatan Street. On entering the Castle Hotel lobby, Ola and his wife realised they had found the ideal scene for the photos. The décor was typical of the 1930s, and Lars Bjuhr, the hotel director, was keen to have ABBA immortalised in the Castle Hotel. All he asked was that the name of the hotel appear in the album credits. It turned out that Stig Anderson and Lars were good friends; they were both music buffs and often went to jazz concerts together.

Polaroïd courtesy of Rune Söderqvist

The art-deco reception of the Castle Hotel was the perfect setting for the new album photographs. Ola Lager's wife began looking for 1930s-style clothes. She went to hire shops for the costumes, and asked friends for accessories and jewellery. Agnetha's green dress was a one-off, tailored for her especially by Hertzbergs Konfektion. Following with the luxury theme

of the Castle Hotel, Ron Spaulding suggested photographing the band in a limousine, and a few days before the photo session, he contacted some luxury car-hire companies, one of which owned a 1952 Rolls-Royce that used to belong to the rich Swedish businessman Torsten Kreuger.

The photo session was set for the end of March at Polar Music, during the lunch break. While the photographer and his assistant set up their equipment around the limousine parked in Nybrogatan Street, the others got ready in the record company's room. Ola's wife was busy preparing clothes, jewellery and accessories, and making sure each of the extras was properly dressed. Lolo Murray, the band's ever-faithful makeup artist, checked their hair and makeup. The four members of ABBA were seated on the back seat of the car and a friend of Ola's took the place of the chauffeur. Rune Söderqvist, who was to become the artistic director of the group some months later, had brought along a leather trunk and lent his white jacket to Björn. As Frida recalled: 'The session in the car didn't last very long because there was no room on the back seat. Björn couldn't even sit down properly!'

Two hours later, they all met up again at the Castle Hotel to finish the photo shoot. Hotel director Lars had set up a buffet for the team in the dining hall. The photographer, his assistant, the makeup artist, the extras, and the hotel staff were all there. The atmosphere was relaxed, but Frida was not feeling well and kept to herself. Among the extras was the photographer's wife

dressed in a long black dress, as well as some friends of theirs, the hotel's receptionist and the bellboy, who was on a two-month training programme at the time and hugely impressed by the experience. To make the scene look more realistic, Ola had Lars Bjuhr stand by the counter pretending to talk on the telephone. As always, Ola took around 100 shots. He added a yellow-orange filter to enhance the retro look of the photos. At the end of the session, Lars asked the photographer to take a few souvenir shots of his wife and children with the band. Everyone changed back into their normal clothes before leaving. Frida, who still felt unwell, decided to go to her dance class all the same, and asked Lars to call her a taxi.

With the album due to go on sale on 21 April, Ola Lager had limited time. The day after the photo session, he collected the photos from the lab and took them to Polar Music. As with the previous album, only two of the photos were to be used for the sleeve. Ola entrusted the finishing touches to his designer-architect friend, Sten-Åke Magnusson, who enhanced the 1930s look with an old-style typeface for the ABBA logo and for the album's texts.

The album ABBA was finally released and exploded onto the Scandinavian music scene. The single 'I Do, I Do, I Do, I Do, I Do' was already on the way up the charts. Although there was less enthusiasm about the album in the UK, it was hugely successful in the rest of Northern Europe. The photos on the album sleeve gave the band a whole new image: no one had ever seen ABBA look so glamorous! However, in a Sweden that was politically to the left, the group was heavily criticised for making middle-class music and for extolling capitalist values by showing themselves in luxury hotels, drinking champagne and driving about in limousines. The Peps Blodsband, an alternative group, even came up with a 'proletarian' version of the ABBA album sleeve.

Ola Lager later replicated the style of the ABBA album sleeve in photos for the Swedish duo Svenne & Lotta and for the orchestra conductor Arthur Greenslade.

Lars Bjuhr bought the Castle Hotel in 1974. Two years later, the ground floor was reconstructed, but the hotel was entirely renovated in 1988. It was renamed Hotel Riddargatan after he sold it in 2001. Jokingly, Lars says, 'Stig forgot to include the Castle Hotel in the album credits, but thanks to your book, it is credited 33 years later!'

(This account of the photo session was made possible thanks to interviews and meetings with Stig Anderson, Ola Lager, Lars Bjuhr, Rune Söderqvist, Ron Spaulding, Sten-Åke Magnusson, Görel Hanser, Frida, Björn and Benny.)

ABBA

'We liked using many styles, from German schlager to Italian ballads, French chansons to the Anglo-Saxon pop world. So we tried our hand at everything, I think.'
BJÖRN

'I Do, I Do, I Do, I Do, I Do' on *Disco* (Germany).

'Interestingly, ABBA have put the finishing touch to their style, becoming more daring and more even. There are no weak songs. Nowadays, it is as easy for Björn and Benny to create smart, easily remembered melodies as it is for others to scratch their heads. OK, the music does not contain great messages, but neither does it claim to. It is music that isn't ashamed to be called *schlager* or pop, and if you compare it to other musicians who work in the same style, then ABBA are superior. Particularly "I Do, I Do, I Do, I Do, I Do", which has to be the best thing they've done, with delightfully foolish saxophones, and a melodic verse and chorus combined with Agnetha's voice, which penetrates through and over Anni-Frid's. Speaking of the girls, it is very possible that Anni-Frid has the "best" voice of the two, but Agnetha's has a special tone, which I find immensely engaging (listen to "I've Been Waiting For You"). I play it often, and so will you.'
Mats Olsson *(Expressen)*

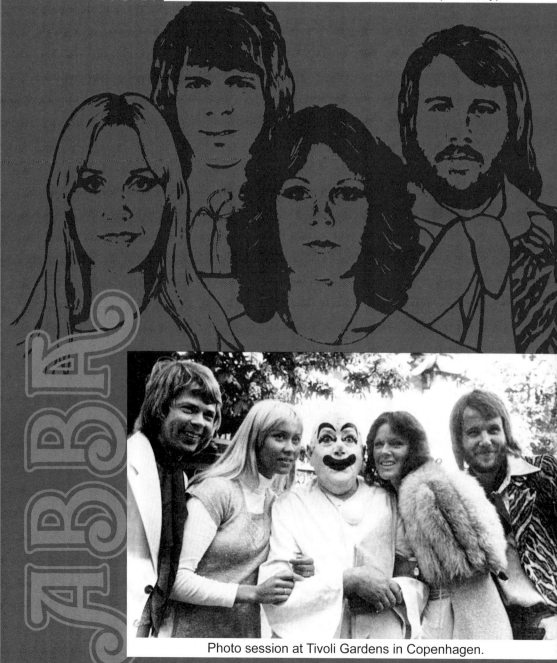

Photo session at Tivoli Gardens in Copenhagen.

In June, ABBA travelled to Hilversum, in Holland, to record *The Eddy Go Round Show*, their first TV special outside Sweden. After the filming of the show, a photo shoot took place in the gardens of the Hooge Vuursche Hotel.

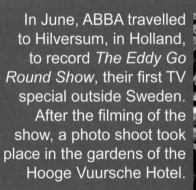

'Frida brought me a picture of a Chinese cat
It really looked like Frida, in fact: beautifu
and a bit wild. That was Frida's image. A
the same time, I had a black Burmese cat a
home named Kissen. Frida agreed to use th
image of Kissen but in a blue colour instea
of black. This is how the whole thing started
the yellow Chinese cat symbol for Frida an
the blue cat Kissen for Agnetha
OWE SANDSTRÖM

'I've always been interested i
fashion. I was very much th
driving force in that chapter
FRID

'Frida wanted something to happen on stage
with the cat dresses. So we decided we would
make them in two pieces: a short tunic and a
long skirt with the yellow or the blue colours
inside. So, all of a sudden, they could just
open it up and drop it. On stage, it really had a
big effect on the audience!' OWE SANDSTRÖM

Lars Wigenius and Owe Sandström.

94

The blue and yellow cat dresses

MADE IN SWEDEN FOR EXPORT

ABBA, Lill Lindfors and Sylvia Vrethammar on the set.

The 45-minute programme *Made In Sweden For Export* was produced by SVT to promote Sweden and its most famous artists abroad. Among them were Björn Skifs, Lill Lindfors, Merit Hemminsson and Sylvia Vrethammar. ABBA performed three songs: 'Mamma Mia', 'I Do, I Do, I Do, I Do, I Do' and 'So Long'. The programme, filmed during Spring 1975, was shown in January 1976 at the MIDEM fair in Cannes and represented Sweden at the Golden Rose of Montreux competition in the spring of the same year.

'So Long'.

'The cat dresses were especially made for the TV programme Made In Sweden For Export. We wanted to use the Swedish colours, blue and yellow, and it was important not to use a piece of the Swedish folklore.'
OWE SANDSTRÖM

'I Do, I Do, I Do, I Do, I Do'.

'Mamma Mia'.

MADE IN SWEDEN FOR EXPORT

97

A break between the soundcheck and the concert at Gröna Lund in Stockholm.

Backstage at Gröna Lund.

The summer tour of the Swedish Folkparks was a triumph with a total of 100,000 spectators. ABBA got excellent reviews.

Champagne after the concert in Skellefteå!

In August, ABBA recorded the *Hei Sveis!* TV programme at Momarkedet in Norway, the largest charity event in Scandinavia, organised annually by the Red Cross. The group performed 'I Do, I Do, I Do, I Do, I Do', 'SOS' and 'Waterloo'.

During the summer, ABBA spent some weeks on their island of Viggsö in the Stockholm archipelago. A time to relax and compose new songs for the next album. A German TV team took this opportunity to make a report on the group including an interview and a very special filmed version of 'SOS' with the group sitting on the rocks near their island home.

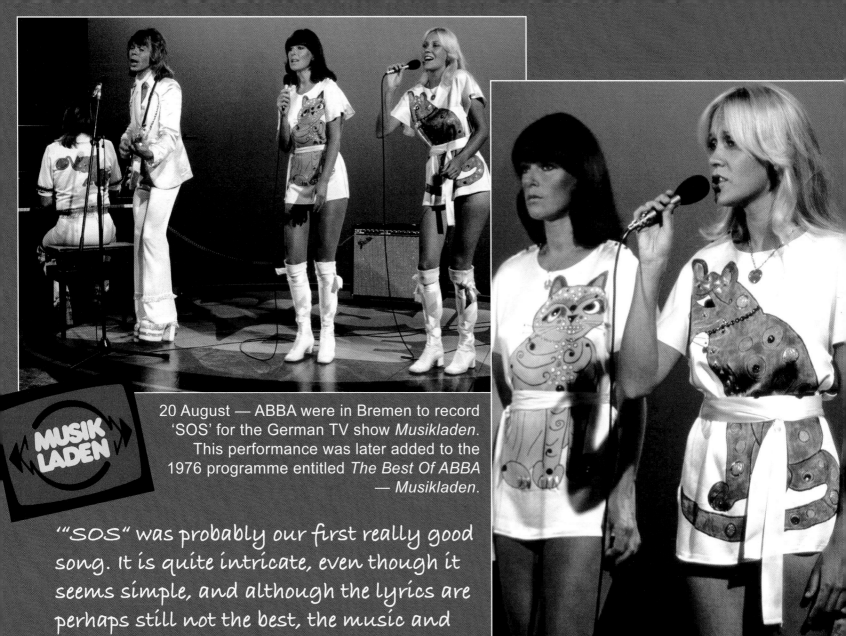

MUSIK LADEN

20 August — ABBA were in Bremen to record 'SOS' for the German TV show *Musikladen*. This performance was later added to the 1976 programme entitled *The Best Of ABBA — Musikladen*.

'"SOS" was probably our first really good song. It is quite intricate, even though it seems simple, and although the lyrics are perhaps still not the best, the music and the actual recording are fine.' BENNY

9 September — Party in a Stockholm restaurant with ABBA, Michael B. Tretow and Svenne & Lotta. Stig presented the group with a platinum disc for sales of the *ABBA* album in Sweden. Svenne & Lotta were given a gold disc for their albums *Svenne & Lotta II* and *Oldies But Goodies*.

ABBA were voted Artists of the Year by readers of Swedish magazine *Vecko Revyn*. At a cocktail party, they were presented with two prizes: a 'fantasy-surrealistic' painting by artist Hans Arnold and an envelope containing a cheque for 5000 Swedish kronors.

Rehearsing 'SOS' on the French TV show *Ring Parade*.

'SOS' on *Top Of The Pops*.

Frida modelling for Swedish magazine *Svensk Damtidning*.

ABBA with American producer Sid Bernstein.

In November, ABBA made a two-week promotional visit to the United States. The group recorded several TV shows in San Diego, Las Vegas, Los Angeles and New York.

NBC's *Saturday Night* show (rehearsals).

NBC's *Saturday Night* show.

Don Kirshner's Rock Concert.

The *Dinah* Shore Show.

At the beginning of December, ABBA were in Germany for the recording of the New Year's Eve show called *Sylvester Tanz Party*. They performed 'I Do, I Do, I Do, I Do, I Do' and 'SOS'.

'It was the Australians who first started to play "Mamma Mia". And consequently that song became a huge hit in Australia, and that kicked off a very strong connection with the fans out there. So from down under comes this noise, and CBS in the UK must have been thinking. "What the hell is this? There is still life in ABBA!"'
BJÖRN

ABBA: Not just a one-hit wonder

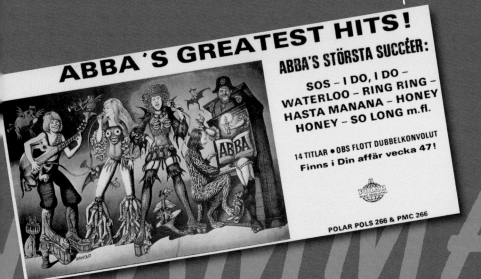

MAMMA MIA

30 August — Anni-Frid took part in the TV show *Sommarnöjet* recorded at Skansen park in Stockholm. She performed 'Aldrig Mej' and 'Syrtaki', two tracks from her forthcoming LP *Frida Ensam* to be released on 10 November.

AKTUELLA SCHLAGER

Nr 141

SVENSKA VISFÖRLAGET
STOCKHOLM

Signing session at Åhléns department store in Stockholm.

Frida ensam

FRIDA ALONE

'Anni-Frid Lyngstad has released a solo LP where her unique and sensual voice comes into its own rather better than when she sings with ABBA. Frida has a musician's ear for phrasing which does itself more justice here than in her tailor-made ABBA songs. *Frida Ensam* is evidently made for mass-market consumption. One wonders if this type of material would have been so predominant if Frida had been given full freedom to decide by herself?'

Hans Fridlund *(Expressen)*

'The album portrays Frida as a very strong and emotive singer and shows the true value of the music, that if sung properly and with enough feeling, it transcends all language barriers. The sleeve photograph is so sensuous that it would make the leaning tower of Pisa stand to attention.'

Harry Doherty *(Melody Maker)*

**Anni-Frid Lyngstad
signerar i dag**

Anni-Frid kommer till city i dag och signerar
sin senaste LP-skiva «Frida ensam».... 37:-
Utgiven på skivmärket Polar.

city 12 - 13, 1 tr.

ÅHLÉNS

ELEVEN WOMEN IN A HOUSE

'I like Agnetha Fältskog. She has a voice that is a pleasure to listen to and that goes straight to my heart. It has done that ever since "Jag Var Så Kär", 1967. So I would like to say that this is a great LP. But I can't. My Agnetha is the Agnetha who sings plaintive ballads, with echoing crescendos, where she has to struggle to make herself heard (she can!). It should be about heart, pain, tears, people who separate, unhappy love and be downright drippingly senti-mental (you see, she can sing songs like that, without them becoming ridiculous. Just like Mireille Mathieu). But this is, of all miseries, a kind of theme LP. Why? To be regarded as "serious"? In that case it would have been better to try harder and open herself to us, instead of allowing a songwriter like Bosse Carl-gren to produce formulaic lyrics from the drawer labelled: "Girls, form 1A". Because this is a musically personal LP (good melodies, good arrangement, a production far from ABBA), that would have been worthy of more genuine and fitting lyrics. On side two they are least in the way and it therefore becomes very good, with songs such as "Mina Ögon", "Dom Har Glömt" (good parts-singing in the chorus, pretty guitar), "Var Det Med Dej?" and "Visa i Åttonde Måna-den", where Agnetha sings absolutely delightfully (good guitar solo, as well). But, next time, skip such ridiculous themes! I want to get to know Agnetha Fältskog rather than a crowd of artificial people in a house that does not exist.'
Mats Olsson *(Expressen)*

Agnetha Fältskog ~
Elva kvinnor i ett hus

Rear of the building located on Bastugatan in Stockholm.

B. Carlgren's original sketch for the album cover.

Agneta Fältskog
ny LP
"elva kvinnor i ett hus"
innehåller S.O.S.
Finns nu på våra skivdiskar.

ÅHLÉNS
TEMPO

If you leave Stockholm and travel in the direction of the Baltic Sea, you have no choice but to cross the archipelago. It is here amongst the 24,000 islands, 25 minutes by boat from the centre of town south of Roslagen, that you find the island of Viggsö. A haven of peace, this is where the group loved to come and recharge their batteries far from the crowds and the media.

Each couple owned their own chalet, as did Stig and his wife Gudrun. Björn and Benny often worked on Viggsö. There were no phones or telex, or anyone to disturb them. The two musicians worked in a little cabin with windows, containing a badly tuned piano. Björn always brought along his guitar and a cassette recorder. Numerous ABBA songs were born on this island, amongst them 'Ring Ring', 'Honey Honey', 'I Do, I Do, I Do, I Do, I Do', 'Tropical Loveland', 'The King Has Lost His Crown' and even the English version of 'Fernando'.

Björn said of Viggsö, 'It's the answer to all the pressure that's put on us. On arriving there, you relax or start working and you feel the stress vanish instantly. We can make music day and night if we want to, without any constraints. I've noticed that, whenever the pace of life becomes too much, I automatically think about Viggsö. It's vital to us. Ultimately it's about putting some water between yourself and the rest of the world in order to find internal peace! People are constantly asking us why we don't leave Sweden so that we can pay less taxes. But we need our roots. We need nature. It's definitely one of the secrets of how we remain level-headed!'

Viewers saw ABBA on the island of Viggsö in certain clips from the Swedish documentary *ABBA-dabba-dooo!!*, filmed during the summer of 1976, and at the end of *ABBA: The Movie*.

VIGGSÖ

A haven of peace

Stig always held parties out on Viggsö for his employees. Christmas and Midsummer celebrations were held out there. He created a warm family feeling between everyone. And there was always music, of course!

Höqnäset

Gr.

Fritidso

Torskholmen

Se

Viggsö

Nyvarp

Byttholmen

Gri

Stora Löknäsholmen

L.

rget

1976

'Dancing Queen' on *The Best Of ABBA — Musikladen Extra*.

'The songs became something of an obsession for us. Each song had to be different, because, in the 60s, that's what the Beatles had done.
The challenge was to not do another "Mamma Mia" or "Waterloo".' BENNY

The year began very well for the group. Their songs were in the charts in numerous countries and they had just won back the British market, often considered to be one of the most difficult to break into in pop music.

Frida broke all records in Sweden with sales of her album *Frida Ensam*. The song 'Fernando' stayed at the top of the charts for nine consecutive weeks and was already being called a Swedish classic.

'Mamma Mia' on *Top Of The Pops*.

The Best of ABBA — *Musikladen Extra* was a TV show filmed by the West German broadcasting company NDR in Bremen. In this special, ABBA performed many of their hits including the first recorded performance of 'Dancing Queen'. 'SOS' (performed on *Musikladen* in August 1975) also appeared. Between the songs, ABBA were interviewed about their career and their lives in Sweden.

Polydor released the double compilation *The Very Best Of ABBA* in August 1976 just before the programme was screened nationwide in Germany.

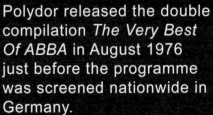

The promo clips for 'Fernando' and 'Dancing Queen' were both filmed at the beginning of February. Lasse Hallström shot the first song in a TV studio with the group singing around a fire. Shooting of 'Dancing Queen' took place at the Alexandra discotheque in Stockholm.

22 February — ABBA were invited to perform 'Fernando' on the *Système 2* show, live from the Sporting Club in Monte-Carlo, the world TV première of the song. A clip of 'Fernando' was also recorded in the Exotic Garden of Monaco. Two days later, the group were in Paris to appear on *Midi-Première*.

FERNANDO

Words and Music by
Benny Andersson, Stig Anderson & Björn Ulvaeus

Recorded on EPIC by

abbainAustralia

Australia, here we come!

During the first half of March, ABBA paid their first visit to Australia. In ten days, the group took part in press conferences, radio interviews and TV shows. One of the high points of this trip was the recording of *The Best Of ABBA*, a 45-minute television special for Channel 9. The reception was as hysterical in Melbourne as it was in Sydney — ABBA had never experienced anything like this before. A newspaper even renamed the nation ABBAustralia!

Press conference at the Sydney Hilton Hotel.

In *The Best Of ABBA*, the group performed eleven songs, with several costume changes. The transmission was a huge event and broke a record in Australia: attracting 54 per cent of the viewers, it was watched by more people than the 1969 moon landing! An overseas version entitled *ABBA In Australia* was produced with additional sequences showing the group at Taronga Zoo and on a cruise on the Hawkesbury River.

On 11 June, Benny and Frida attended Lars Berghagen's wedding.

'Fernando' on *Top of the Pops*.

'"Dancing Queen" is one of our three best songs, and it means a lot for the gay movement. It is still playing at the discotheques. The King and Queen Silvia looked very pleased up on their balcony at their wedding in 1976. But Silvia should not think that it is written for her . . .' (laughs). BJÖRN

Dress rehearsal.

On 18 June, ABBA were invited to perform at a televised gala in celebration of the wedding of King Carl XVI Gustaf of Sweden to Silvia Sommerlath. They were the only pop act to appear in the show and, although it hadn't been written for the occasion, they chose to perform the obvious song 'Dancing Queen', dressed in baroque outfits appropriate for the gala transmitted from The Royal Swedish Opera in Stockholm.

Frida backstage.

'The day that Benny and I finished mixing the instrumental track of "Dancing Queen", I was so excited, I just could not rest. Agnetha was asleep and I just had to share it with someone, so I drove all over Stockholm looking for someone to play it to. Finally I ended up at my sister's house. I played it over and over again to her. We couldn't believe how good it sounded.' BJÖRN

ABBA®

The designer and artist Rune Söderqvist started working with ABBA in 1975, designing the original Swedish sleeve for their *Greatest Hits* album. In 1976, he created the famous ABBA logo with the inverted B. His thinking was that each B (Björn and Benny) should be turned towards each A (Agnetha and Anni-Frid) since they were two couples. Rune went on to design every subsequent album sleeve from *Arrival* up to *ABBA Live* in 1986. He was also the stage designer for ABBA's tours in 1977 and 1979. Rune and his common-law wife, Lillebil Ankarcrona, were close friends of Frida and Benny.

'Dancing Queen' was the first record to feature the group's distinctive mirror-image logo (with the first 'B' reversed).

'"Dancing Queen" has a disco feel, but it's a bit slow to hustle to. Great just to listen to, though! One of their best yet! We've become accustomed to these super-commercial productions from this band of greats. The single grows and grows. A huge hit!'
Caroline Coon *(Melody Maker)*

DANCING QUEEN

ABBA in advertising

National Colour TV
CL-2621L
Type 26—63cm Diagonal 110" "In-Line" colour TV with both

National Colour TV
TC-2002
Type 20—48cm Diagonal Quintrix "In-Line" colour TV with both VHF and UHF tuners

National

In 1976, ABBA took part in a huge advertising campaign for the Japanese electronics manufacturer National. Stig and the four members of the group signed a $A1 million deal which was used to offset the costs of the Australian tour the following March. ABBA recorded new lyrics to their tune 'Fernando' and five commercials were filmed in Stockholm in August.

Lots of companies wanted to use the name of ABBA in their advertising but Stig Anderson was always against it. He made an exception for the brands National, Lois and Blaupunkt.

"Vi är kräsna på ljud, därför valde vi Blaupunkt bilradio i våra bilar"

... säger ABBA.

● BLAUPUNKT
BOSCH gruppen

... ljud, finns det bara en bilradio: Blaupunkt!

● BLAUPUNKT
BOSCH gruppen

MEMBER OF Lois
JEANS & JACKETS FAMILY

The Polar Music offices

INSIDE THE WONDERFUL WORLD OF ABBA

Baldersgatan 1, in the embassy district of Stockholm. ABBA's headquarters moved here during the summer of 1975. Renovation, supervised by Stig's wife Gudrun, had cost a great deal of time and money but the result was a pleasant and modern workplace with several offices, a rehearsal room, a meeting room to receive journalists, the fan club's office and a sauna with relaxation room. There was a family feeling amongst the nineteen Polar and Sweden Music employees and Stig placed a lot of importance on the family way in which the business was run.

Björn, Görel and Agnetha.

Lunch with two lucky fans.

Ready to meet the journalists!

ABBA dabba dooo!!

For the first time, Swedish Television dedicated a whole programme to ABBA. The documentary, entitled *ABBA-dabba-Dooo!!*, coincided with the release of the new *Arrival* album and showed a different side of the group. Each member of ABBA was interviewed, short film clips were made for some of the songs and the group performed two tracks, live with an orchestra.

abba

7-8 October — ABBA were invited to go to Poland where they had been named Most Popular Group in Eastern Europe. The Polish government chartered an 'ABBA Special' plane to bring them to Warsaw, together with a hundred European journalists. Following a press conference and a tour of the Polish capital, ABBA recorded a 45-minute TV special entitled *ABBA In Studio 2*.

inPoland

Agnetha came with her father Ingvar.

ABBA
in the USA

In October, ABBA took off for a two-week visit to the USA and Canada (Los Angeles, Vancouver, New York and Philadelphia). They did the usual round of interviews with press and radio and took part in several TV shows. Atlantic Records promoted the *Greatest Hits* album and proclaimed a 'National ABBA Weekend' to capitalise on the group's visit.

The group appeared on several TV shows: *Midnight Special*, *Don Kirshner's Rock Concert*, *Dinah!*, *The Wolfman Jack Show*, the *CBC Television Special*, *Wonderama* and *The Mike Douglas Show*.

On 11 October, the long-awaited *Arrival* album was finally released. Although it was heavily criticised for its weak lyrics, the album is considered to be one of ABBA's best records. It proved how much the group had developed both musically and artistically. *Arrival* transformed ABBA from Swedish pop curiosity to worldwide phenomenon.

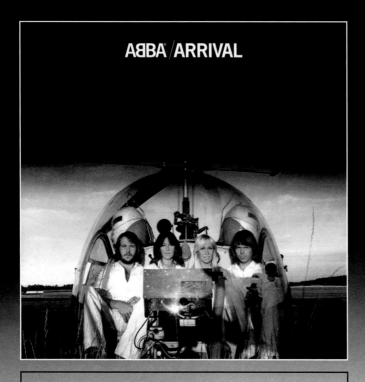

'Stig, who understood how powerful the new logo could be, asked me to put it at the top of the record sleeve. This would mean that ABBA's albums could be instantly found on the shelves of the record stores.'
RUNE SÖDERQVIST

'There is no doubt that ABBA are the classiest pop outfit around Europe at the moment. Björn Ulvaeus and Benny Andersson write snappy commercial tunes. ABBA, and in particular, the vocalists, Frida and Agnetha, strengthen the identity with tight vocal interpretations, backed by a cool continental instrumental sound. That is the base from which ABBA operate, rarely venturing outside strictly defined terms of reference. A toe-tapping tune, a simple, sing-a-long lyric. Short and direct that is the ABBA sound. That is *Arrival*. Ironically, although the album is initially impressive by its forthright and innocent out-and-about pop, after a while the clinical aspect of the construction of an ABBA song becomes increasingly annoying. I've had this album for a few weeks and played it a lot. It is only now, after my sixth or seventh listen, that the coldness of the structure is beginning to rub me the wrong way.'
Harry Doherty *(Melody Maker)*

'The title Arrival was suggested by Lillebil, my common-law wife at the time. The idea of the helicopter came quickly as soon as we got the title of the album. I previously had had the idea of shooting at the North Pole. Everything was arranged for the photo session but we had to stop that project because Agnetha refused to fly.'
RUNE SÖDERQVIST

ABBA *in the* UK

Mid-November, ABBA travelled to England for four days where Epic-CBS had planned a massive promotional campaign. A grand reception with press conference and luncheon awaited the four Swedes on the *Mayflower*, a ship anchored on the River Thames. BBC DJ Simon Bates presented ABBA with 32 gold, platinum and silver discs for the group's sales in Britain, plus a diamond disc for the fabulous sales of *Greatest Hits*.

Press conference at the Bel Air Hotel , The Hague.

In November, Benny and Frida left their flat in the old town part of Stockholm to move into a villa on the island of Lidingö.

Een van de Acht TV show — rehearsals.

ABBA were invited to take part in the Dutch TV show *Een van de Acht*, hosted by Mies Bouwman, on which they performed three songs. Before the recording, the four Swedes were presented with numerous gold and platinum discs at a press conference in The Hague.

money, money, money

Les Rendez-Vous du Dimanche — Paris.

SKIV-spegeln

1	(1)	Arrival — ABBA 13	
2	(2)	Take the heat of me — Boney M 10	
3	(3)	Varning för barn — Magnus & Bras	
		Saxparty III — Ingemar Nordström	
4	(4)	Dance little lady — Tina Charles 9	
5	(7)	A new world record — Electric L	
6	(8)	Orchestra 5	
		A day at the races — Queen 2	
		Dr Hook 22	

British Top 50

1	20 GOLDEN GREATS, Glen Campbell
2	ARRIVAL, Abba
5	100 GOLDEN GREATS, Max Bygraves
3	DISCO ROCKET, Various
—	HOTEL CALIFORNIA, The Eagles
4	GREATEST HITS OF, Frankie Valli and the Fou
10	GREATEST HITS, Abba
—	A DAY AT THE RACES, Queen
9	A NEW WORLD RECORD, Electric Light Orch
8	

The Dancing KINGS and QUEENS!

THE rise and rise of Swedish singing group, Abba, has been nothing less than phenomenal. All but one of their records reached the number one spot in 1976, and things only look like improving, judging by the success 1977 has already brought them!

Songs such as "I Do, I Do, I "Dancing Queen" are and all

ABBA ARRIVAL

1976 was a year of great success and one of the most important of ABBA's career. Rehearsals for the forthcoming tour began in December at Grünewaldsalen, in Stockholm. In Britain, the group's popularity was obvious when the two concerts at the London's Royal Albert Hall were announced: the organisers received 3.5 million ticket applications for the 11,212 seats available!

Recording a five-part radio series with Ulf Elfving.

1977 TOUR

the magic of ABBA

'GORILLAS' AT EVERY ABBA DOOR

Abba will be surrounded by exceedingly tight security during their Australian tour, with "a gorilla at every door."

By PHIL SCOTT

"We have what I describe as a mini rock opera in the stage show and maybe we could expand that idea. So long as we

★ABBA★
EN PUBLIC ET EN COULEURS

ABBA
ON TOUR/ARRIVAL

2.2. Berlin, Deutschlandhalle · 3.2. Köln, Sporthalle · 6.2. Essen, Grugahalle
7.2. Hannover, Eilenrieder Halle · 8.2. Hamburg, CCH

© Universaltryck Grafiska AB

ABBA ARRIVAL

Polydor © 2344 058 · 3226 058
Abba - Arrival
Side 1: When I Kissed The Teacher -
Dancing Queen - My Love, My Life - Dum
Dum Diddle - Knowing Me, Knowing You
Side 2: Money, Money, Money
That's Me - Why Did It Have To Be Me -
Tiger - Arrival

ON TOUR WITH
ABBA

Brøndby-Hallen
man. 31. jan. kl. 19.30
Knud Thorbjørnsen & EMA proudly present
ABBA

City Billetbureau
Mikkel Bryggers Gade.
Tlf. (01) 11 24 65 og (01) 13 45 31.
Billetkøen 0066

© Universaltryck Grafiska AB

TOEGANGSPRIJS incl.
Belasting op
20%/0 Vermakelijkh.

f 25.00

ABBA® 41219

Cont. 4 Febr. 8.00 u.
JAAP EDENHAL 7 1219

Abba risk lives singing in the rain

FRIDA

Abba risked their lives to play at last night's rain-swept concert at Sydney

AGNETHA'S BOTTOM TOPS SHOW

That admirable piece of ...tom ...declared a Swedish national ...al ...boredom ...

...ndag ...n. 1977

ABBA
IN CONCERT

ROYAL ALBERT HALL
General Manager: ANTHONY J. CHARLTON

Monday 14 February, 1977
at 9.00 p.m. Doors open at 8.30
ALEC LESLIE and HARVEY GOLDSMITH
in association with KNUD THORBJØRNSEN presents
ABBA in Concert

STALLS **K**

973
RETAINED

£7.50

Enter...

ABBA

...ertages ej.

SEKTION **D**
HÖGER

SITT-PLATS KR	RAD	PLATS
30:—	19	26

...NDINAVIUM

The first leg of the tour started in Oslo, Norway, on 28 January, and continued to Sweden, Denmark, Germany, Holland, Belgium and Great Britain, concluding with two concerts at London's Royal Albert Hall on 14 February.

The four Swedes offered the audiences a spectacular two-hour stage show featuring 25 songs and the 'mini-musical' *The Girl With The Golden Hair*. Both stage and costumes were predominantly white, with blue curtains and large vases filled with red silk roses. The costumes, designed by Owe Sandström, were brightened up with golden trimmings.

Arrival in Oslo.

Frida leaving her handprints in cement at Gothenburg's amusement park.

'I always thought Frida was much better on stage. She had more control over her body. Somehow she was a strong character. On stage, we were competing for the audience but we helped each other very much.'

AGNETHA

OSLO
GOTHENBURG
COPENHAGEN
BERLIN
COLOGNE
AMSTERDAM
ANTWERP
ESSEN
HANOVER
HAMBURG
BIRMINGHAM
MANCHESTER
GLASGOW

ABBA LIVE

'I think it's dead fun being onstage. That's where I experience the happiest moments of my life. When I stand there I'm completely na-ked and open. I turn myself inside out and have nothing against expo-sing myself. I feel secure because I enjoy what I'm doing.'

FRIDA

'To be on tour all the time is terribly demanding, both physically as well as psychologically.'

BENNY

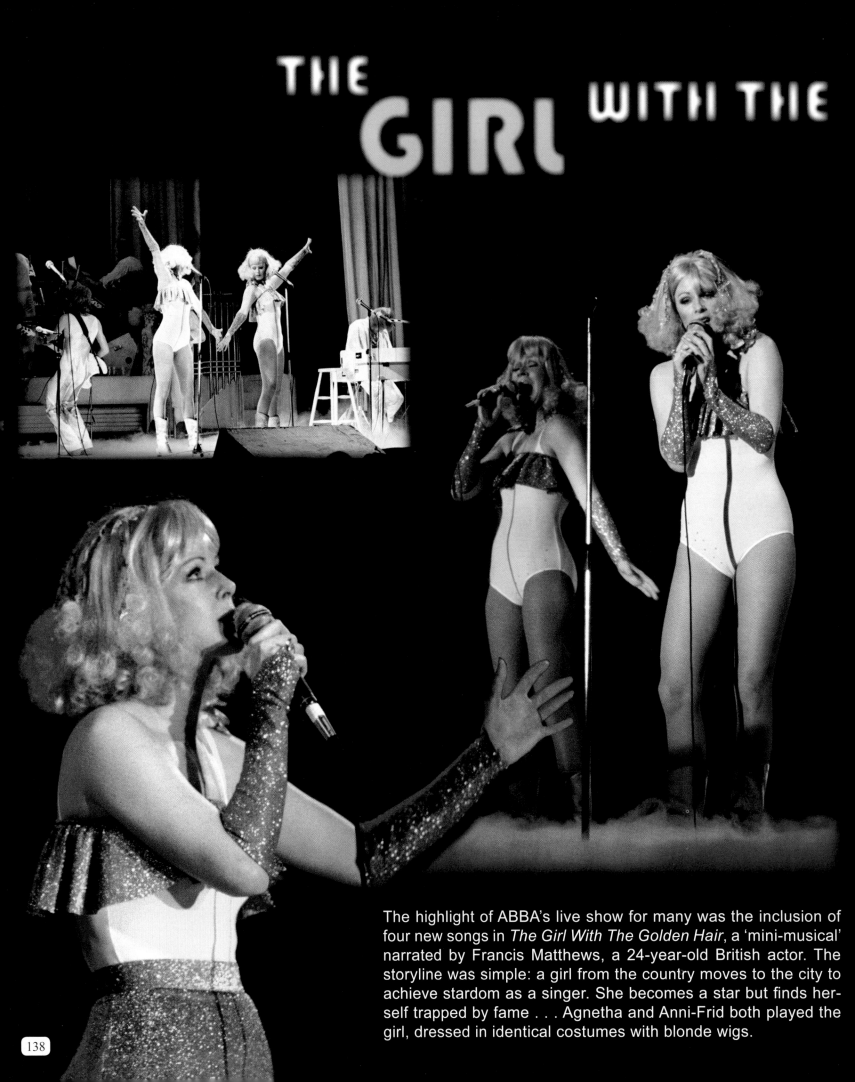

THE GIRL WITH THE

The highlight of ABBA's live show for many was the inclusion of four new songs in *The Girl With The Golden Hair*, a 'mini-musical' narrated by Francis Matthews, a 24-year-old British actor. The storyline was simple: a girl from the country moves to the city to achieve stardom as a singer. She becomes a star but finds herself trapped by fame . . . Agnetha and Anni-Frid both played the girl, dressed in identical costumes with blonde wigs.

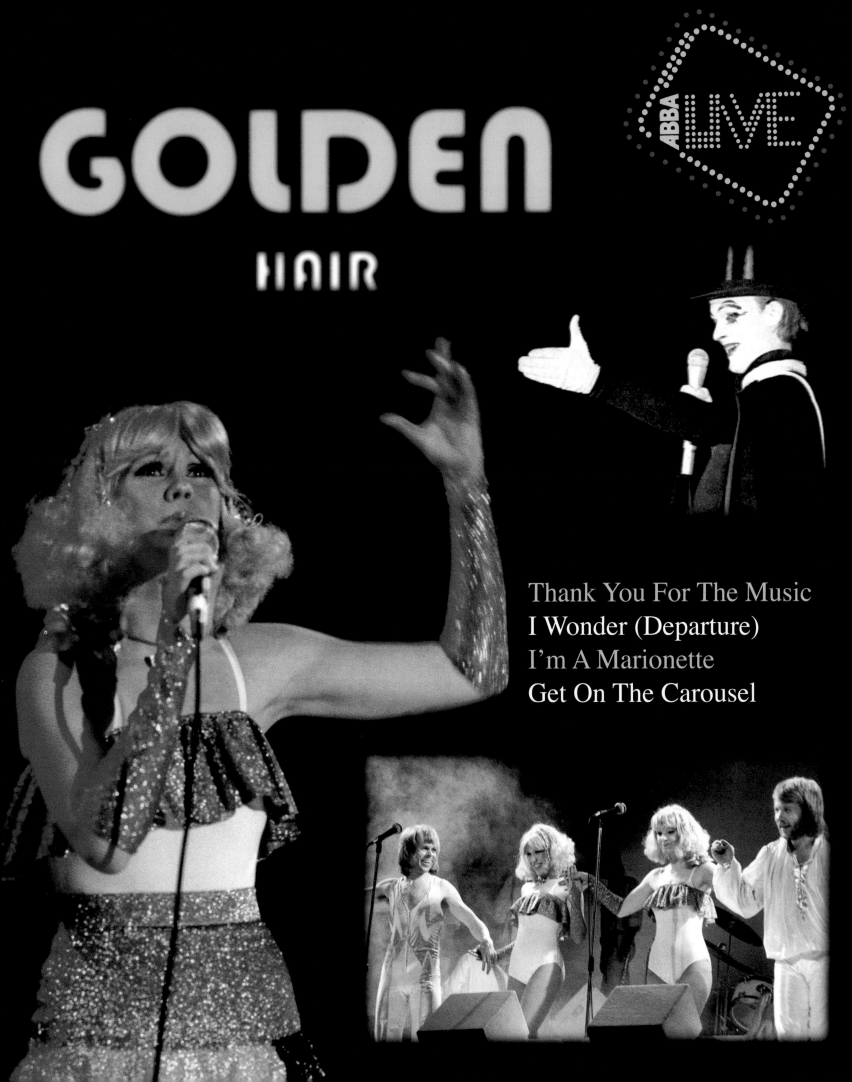

GOLDEN HAIR

ABBA LIVE

Thank You For The Music
I Wonder (Departure)
I'm A Marionette
Get On The Carousel

Press conference at the Sebel Town House in Sydney.

A swim in the Swan River in Perth.

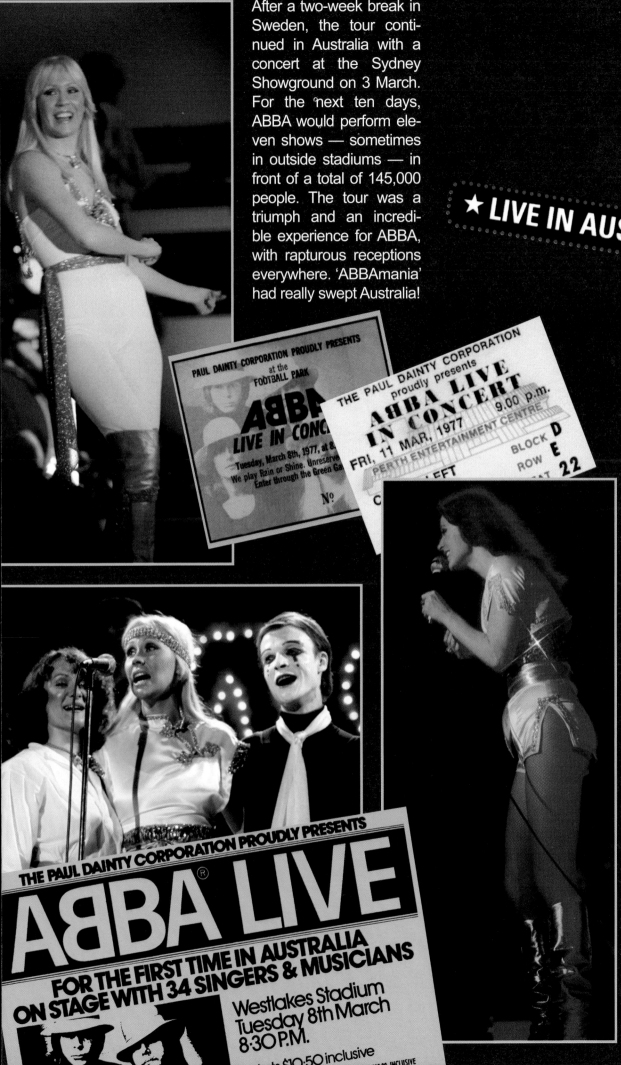

After a two-week break in Sweden, the tour continued in Australia with a concert at the Sydney Showground on 3 March. For the next ten days, ABBA would perform eleven shows — sometimes in outside stadiums — in front of a total of 145,000 people. The tour was a triumph and an incredible experience for ABBA, with rapturous receptions everywhere. 'ABBAmania' had really swept Australia!

★ LIVE IN AUSTRALIA - 1977 ★

SYDNEY
MELBOURNE
ADELAIDE
PERTH

PAUL DAINTY CORPORATION PROUDLY PRESENTS
at the
FOOTBALL PARK
ABBA
LIVE IN CONC
Tuesday, March 8th, 1977, at 8
We play Rain or Shine. Unreserve
Enter through the Green Ga
Nº

THE PAUL DAINTY CORPORATION
proudly presents
ABBA LIVE
IN CONCERT
FRI, 11 MAR, 1977   9.00 p.m.
PERTH ENTERTAINMENT CENTRE
BLOCK   D
ROW   E
LEFT   22

'That tour was madness. I think that for a couple of years afterwards we went stone cold in Australia. We had been overexposed. But luckily the fan base came back. The tour itself was an extraordinary, wonderful experience.' BENNY

THE PAUL DAINTY CORPORATION PROUDLY PRESENTS
ABBA LIVE
FOR THE FIRST TIME IN AUSTRALIA
ON STAGE WITH 34 SINGERS & MUSICIANS
Westlakes Stadium
Tuesday 8th March
8:30 P.M.
$10.50 inclusive

Agnetha and Björn had recently moved from their first villa to a new home, still located on the island of Lidingö.

After a very hectic year, it was decided that at the end of the tour ABBA would spend most of the year resting and recording the new album. Stig declared, 'ABBA are not available for anything from April to October.'

The single 'Knowing Me, Knowing You' was released in February. A few weeks earlier, the group had recorded the promotional clip with Lasse Hallström in wintry Stockholm and in a studio for the indoor shots.

knowing me, knowing you

1977

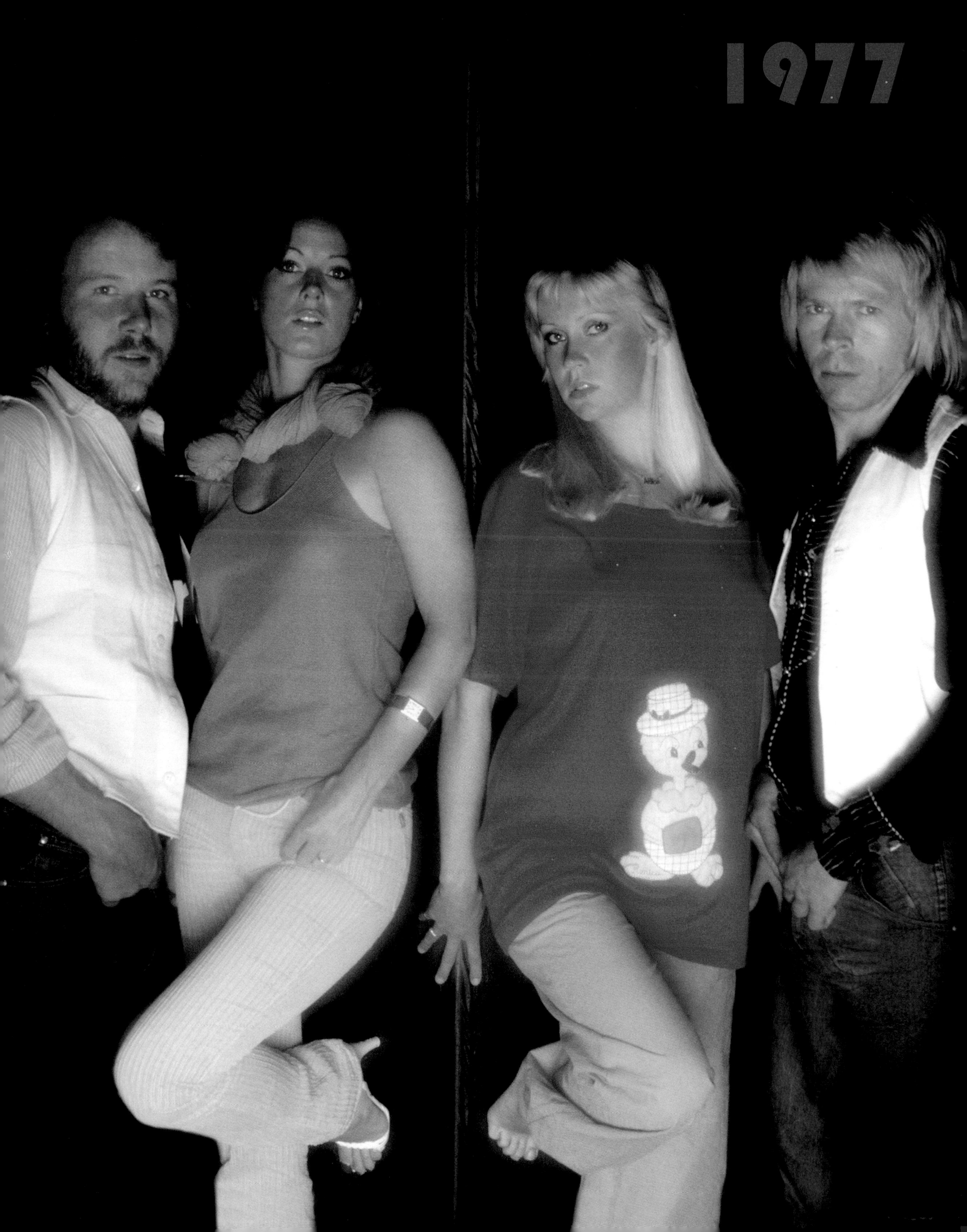

'Dancing Queen' reached No. 1 in the United States on 9 April. For Björn and Benny, it was a dream come true. A few weeks later, they travelled to Los Angeles with Michael B. Tretow to meet Tom Hidley, whose mission was to equip ABBA's future recording studio, which was to be built in an old Stockholm cinema, the Riverside.

Back in Sweden, Björn and Benny began recording the new album at Marcus Music Studio with the backing track of 'A Bit Of Myself' which was to become 'The Name Of The Game'.

After a break to film the additional scenes for *ABBA: The Movie* in Stockholm, Björn and Benny got back to work and alternated writing and studio recording sessions throughout the summer.

Agnetha and Björn announced to the press that they were expecting their second child at the end of the year.

Lill Babs and Frida backstage before Lasse Berghagen's show at Gröna Lund in Stockholm.

Recording the new album

The new album was recorded and mixed at Marcus Music Studio and Metronome Studio in Stockholm, between May and November 1977. The track 'The Name Of The Game' was mixed in September at Bohus Studio in Kungälv, near Gothenburg, on the west coast of Sweden.

Recording sessions were both hectic and stressful for the group as the album was planned for release in conjunction with the movie at the end of the year. With the added difficulty of the heavily pregnant Agnetha only being able to attend recording sessions during mornings, it seemed that the release date should be postponed. But, with a lot of hard work, the group actually managed to meet the deadline in Scandinavia, where *ABBA: The Album* was released on 12 December.

'It isn't easy to discover that you have a father, in the middle of your grown-up life. I have lived without him for so long and believed he was dead. No one can force us to have any feelings. It's something that has to develop over time.' FRIDA

Frida attended the Swedish première of the new James Bond film *The Spy Who Loved Me* on 17 September.

Beginning of September, Frida was reunited with her father, Alfred Haase, thanks to an article published in the German pop magazine *Bravo*.

THE NAME OF THE GAME/I WONDER (Departure)

'"The Name Of The Game" doesn't have the immediate impact of many of ABBA's other songs, but in its build-up and delivery improves each time you hear it. It is a quiet song lacking the compact sound that characterised "Dancing Queen". Here you hear more of each instrument separately, and it is the bass that drives the song forward. On top of the slightly sluggish rhythm, the parts-singing that has become ABBA's trademark is built. At the end comes a somewhat compressed but nevertheless distinctive guitar. The best part of the song is the slightly melancholy melody, and the two occasions when the group pause and sing "doa" without accompaniment. The worst is a shrill trumpet that recalls too much of the Beatles' "Penny Lane" period to be any good. This is a partially new ABBA sound, even more evident on the B-side "I Wonder", recorded on stage in Sydney. It's a very pretty ballad that was a part of the group's "Mini-Musical". Frida sings it with feeling and they make use of the choir perfectly, together with the string section that strengthened ABBA's music during the Australian tour. The song possesses the same positive qualities as the best "real" musical melodies and shows that, as composers, Björn and Benny are not trying to drive on the same tracks, but rather always seeking to extend and renew their sound. It's a good single.'

Mats Olsson (*Expressen*)

'Do you have
a newspaper
with nothing
about
ABBA?'

The Swedish daily newspaper *Expressen* paid homage to ABBA with the first in a series of cartoon strips retracing the group's career. The idea and texts came from Peter Himmelstrand and the pictures were drawn by Kjell Ekeberg.

On 4 December, Agnetha gave birth to her second child, a boy named Christian Peter.

Promo gold flexi disc from Sweden.

Benny and Frida on the Swedish TV programme *Nöjesliv*.

The Swedish première of *ABBA: The Movie* took place at the China cinema in Stockholm, on 26 December. After the screening of the film, the four Swedes were presented with a golden gong.

'This review will not refer to the anatomies of female ABBA members. What it will refer to is the (partly) superb new record from the group . . . ABBA on record shows up all their best features — their songwriting talent, their instrumental proficiency, their ability as arrangers, their vocal precision, without uncovering their worst — their clumsy stage presence, their lack of humour, their showbiz shoddiness. *The Album* can be divided into two separate sections, side one and side two. Side one is a further development of the ABBA tradition of great pop singles. Side two is a different kettle of fish — a signpost to their possible future direction, a move which lays bare ABBA's ambitions, pretensions, and, unintentionally, their limitations . . . ABBA then proceed to discard any connections they might have had with rock music by performing "Three Scenes From A Mini-Musical". And this is where they come horribly unstuck. ABBA's lyrics have never been their strongest point, understandably perhaps, since they're writing in a foreign language, but as long as they stick to pop tunes that doesn't matter too much — lots of pop classics have had truly dreadful lyrics, and it didn't matter at all. But when you take it upon yourself to write a musical, it's a different matter. To make a successful musical, you need a plot, you need some credible characters, and you need at least a modicum of wit and humour in the lyrics. ABBA's mini-musical "The Girl With The Golden Hair" has none of these.'

Sheila Prophet *(Record Mirror)*

ABBA: The Album was first released in Scandinavia on 12 December. The rest of the world had to wait a few weeks before the LP reached their local record shops. *ABBA: The Album* was a major international hit in 1978.

'From the very start, Stig Anderson wanted the album to promote the film and the film to promote the album. It was therefore necessary to create something which was relevant to them both. I thought that it would be original not to just feature a photo of the group but to use the contents of the film as an illustration. Firstly, I did a sketch of the four ABBA members' heads, which Björn Andersson then painted. I added to that all the tiny characters from the film.'

RUNE SÖDERQVIST

ABBATHEMOVIE

As it had been decided that ABBA would not tour during 1978, Stig and the group spent a lot of time discussing the idea of making a film of the concerts that could function as a television special. Preliminary shooting was done at the London Royal Albert Hall, but the project had grown into an ambitious full-length film in Panavision. Swedish filmmaker Lasse Hallström, who had directed all of ABBA's promo clips, was naturally chosen to shape *ABBA: The Movie*. Australian production company Reg Grundy supplied 25 per cent of the budget while Polar Music financed the rest. Lasse, who has always considered concert films to be boring, decided that the film would work better if it had some kind of plot. To add an element of humour and continuity, Hallström devised an essentially simple story featuring actors including Robert Hughes, Bruce Barry and Tom Oliver.

'The film is really meant to be an equivalent for an ABBA tour in 1978.'
BJÖRN

A considerable amount of *ABBA: The Movie* was shot during the two weeks ABBA spent in Australia. Several songs were filmed at each concert. However, many clips were shot at the Entertainment Centre in Perth, as it had better acoustics than in the other outside stadiums. Numerous sequences were filmed during the daytime (airports, stadiums, press conferences, interviews with fans) and many ideas for scenes were thought up and improvised on the spot. After ABBA left Perth, the film crew stayed in Australia to film some additional scenes with the actors, as well as location footage such as the Moomba parade in Melbourne.

ABBA
The Making of The Movie!

Robert Hughes

Shooting for the additional scenes continued in Stockholm and the surrounding area. Actors Robert Hughes and Tom Oliver flew over especially from Australia. Among several scenes filmed in the Swedish capital were the hotel-room sequence staged at Stockholm's Sheraton Hotel, Ashley's dream sequence during 'The Name Of The Game' and the scenes in the hotel elevator.

Lasse Hallström

Tom Oliver

'Looking back on ABBA: The Movie, it was really like a film school to me, to play around with all the equipment we had.'
LASSE HALLSTRÖM

A break during the filming of Ashley's dream sequence on the island of Djurgården.

'The girls were dead scared of speaking English on screen.
They just didn't want to do it.'
BJÖRN

ABBA
The Making of The Movie!

Preparing for filming the elevator sequence.

Post-production

In July, Lasse Hallström, Malou Hallström and Ulf Neidemar set to work on editing the movie. The 50 hours of film shot in Australia, plus the additional Stockholm footage, had to be condensed down to 90 minutes. Once the film had been edited and the final choice of songs determined, Björn and Benny began work on the film soundtrack. Extensive re-recording of the live tracks was done during the second half of September at Bohus Studio in Kungälv, on the west coast of Sweden.

Ashley Wallace, a young country music radio DJ from Sydney, is assigned to secure an exclusive in-depth interview with ABBA during their Australian tour. Inexperienced and without his press card, he finds it impossible to break through the barricade of bodyguards surrounding the group. After following ABBA from city to city, he finally meets the four 'inaccessible' Swedish stars by chance in a hotel lift. Exhausted but happy, he makes it back to the radio station just in time to broadcast his report. As it goes out on the air, ABBA are leaving Australia, at the end of their triumphant tour.

Abba : du poivre sous le sucre

Swedish, sexy...and so clean

Appetising Abba delight

Another hit for Abba

ABBA: The Movie turned out to be a box-office success in 1978, in Europe. In the UK, it was the seventh most successful film of the year, after *Star Wars*, *Grease* and *Saturday Night Fever*. In Australia, the film had been successful, although not to the extent that the producers hoped for. It seemed that ABBA fever had died down. In America, where *ABBA: The Movie* opened in the autumn of 1979, the film failed to become a box-office smash.

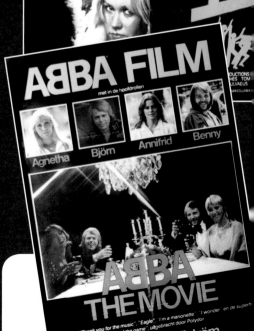

During the first weeks of 1978, the four members of ABBA went into hibernation. While Björn, Benny, Frida and Stig went to the MIDEM music market in Cannes to promote the film and the new album, Agnetha stayed at home and devoted her time to her newborn baby Christian.

Björn, Frida and Benny in Cannes.

During a short interview in the French *Loto Parade* TV programme.

'We hated touring, and we were always careful never to be away from Linda and Christian for more than a few days. But for Agnetha, it was really hard.

BJÖRN

A CHANCE ON M

Stig Anderson is happy to invite you to a private showing of "ABBA-The Movie" at

....

on Monday January 23rd at ....

Polar Music International AB / Disks Melba / Warner-Columbia Film

RSVP before January 17th to Polar Music International AB, P.O. Fack, S-100 41 Stockholm 26, Sweden, telex 11959.

PS. Please bring this invitation with you.

ABBA® THE MOVIE

Stig Anderson est heureux de vous inviter a la projection privée du film « ABBA-The Movie » au cinema ....

....

le lundi 23 janvier à ....

Polar Music International AB / Disks Melba / Warner-Columbia Film

RSVP avant le 17 janvier à Polar Music International AB, P.O. Fack, S-100 41 Stockholm 26, Sweden, telex 11959.

PS. N'oubliez pas de prendre cette invitation avec vous, s'il vous plait.

At the Polar Music offices before an interview for Swiss television.

1978

ABBA's visit to launch ABBA: The Movie in Britain was packed with activity: as well as the première, the group were presented with the Carl Alan Award by Princess Margaret, were interviewed by BB Radio One DJ Dave Lee Travis, filmed a TV commercial for ABB The Album and appeared on the Blue Peter TV show.

Keith Moon (The Who) attended the première.

Princess Margaret presenting the Carl Alan Award.

GALA PREMIERE

ABBA® THE MOVIE

on Thursday 16th February 1978 at 8·15 for 8·45pm at the Warner West End, Leicester Square W.C.2.

Dress optional   Performance ends approx.10·25pm

Doors open 8·00pm   STALLS   Row B   Seat   13

162

'Take A Chance On Me' (rehearsals).

BREMEN

On Rudi Carrell's show, ABBA took part in games and interviews.

ABBA, who were unable to attend the German première of ABBA: The Movie, took part in the TV show Am Laufenden Band, presented by Rudi Carrell. Anni-Frid's father, Alfred Haase, also participated in the programme. During their two-day visit to Germany, the four Swedes were presented with various awards from teenage magazines, voted for by their readers.

Alfred Haase with Frida.

Agnetha and Björn presented the ABBA Prize trophy to seven-year-old Agnetha Hjort at a junior skiing competition which the group had sponsored in 1978. The event had been named the ABBA Prize, with the winner receiving a trophy and a cheque for 100,000 Swedish kronors.

Two of the ABBA dolls released by the toy company Matchbox.

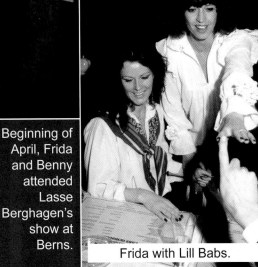

Beginning of April, Frida and Benny attended Lasse Berghagen's show at Berns.

Frida with Lill Babs.

The Swedish Tourist Office launched a massive campaign, featuring ABBA, to promote Sweden overseas.

PARIS

Mid-April, ABBA travelled to Paris for several days of promotional work. They recorded the show *Les Rendez-Vous du Dimanche* with Michel Drucker, who dedicated half of his programme to the group and the release of their film, entitled *Vive ABBA*, in France.

LOS ANGELES

Four Swedish stars on Sunset Boulevard.

In 1978, ABBA made a serious effort to conquer the United States. Stig signed a contract with the American 'starmakers' Scotti Brothers, and May was proclaimed ABBA Month by Atlantic Records to give the group a big promotional push. ABBA flew to Los Angeles and appeared as special guests in an Olivia Newton-John television special.

ABBA with Andy Gibb and Olivia Newton-John.

Polar Music Studios in Stockholm

Built in the old Rivoli Cinema — later the Riverside Cinema — on Sankt Eriksgatan in Stockholm, Polar Music Studios was one of the most technologically advanced studios in the world. After the inauguration in May 1978, word spread rapidly in the music community. Led Zeppelin had already showed up in December 1978 to record their last studio album *In Through The Out Door*, and were followed by the likes of Roxy Music, Earth Wind & Fire, the Ramones, Genesis, the Pretenders, Backstreet Boys, the Rolling Stones and almost every major Swedish musician of the past 30 years. ABBA recorded their last three albums *Voulez Vous*, *Super Trouper* and *The Visitors* here. The studios closed their doors in 2004 after 26 years of operation. Polar Music Studios is considered by many to be as legendary as Abbey Road Studios, where the Beatles recorded.

During the summer ABBA took a seven-week holiday — Benny and Frida went to Barbados while Björn and Agnetha stayed with the children on the island of Viggsö. The two couples returned to work at the beginning of August for what was their first proper session in the new Polar Music Studios. ABBA continued work on their next album and put the finishing touches to the new single 'Summer Night City'.

'"Summer Night City" was a really good song but it never came out right. We tried it and tried it, and we had 50 mixes of it. It's still a good song and it's a fairly good recording, but not the way it was supposed to be. It could have been much better!' MICHAEL B. TRETOW

SUMMER NIGHT CITYSUMMER NIGHT CITYSUMM

PARIS

18 October — ABBA flew to Paris for two days of promotion. Their second visit of the year to the French capital was centred around the recording of the daily TV show *Top Club*. The four Swedes were guests of honour the following week so they re-corded six songs in one evening. During their stay, ABBA did a lot of shopping on the Champs-Elysées and had dinner with Mireille Mathieu at the famous restaurant Le Grand Véfour.

Press conference at the Hilton Tokyo Hotel.

Mid-November, ABBA arrived in Japan. They stayed ten days in Tokyo but the timetable was very tight. The group met the press, took part in several TV and radio shows and recorded an *ABBA Special* for television. A week after their visit, they got their first Japanese No. 1 hit with 'Summer Night City'.

Mike Yarwood in good company!

After a nine-year engagement, Benny and Frida finally married on Friday, 6 October in the Lidingö church, near their own home. The ceremony took place surrounded by as much secrecy as possible, with only three people present: the priest and the two witnesses — the verger and Bitte, Benny and Frida's housekeeper. The couple invited 25 of their friends to a party at their villa the following day.

On 6 December, the two couples flew to London where they were scheduled to tape television appearances on the *Mike Yarwood Christmas Show* and *Jim'll Fix It*. On *Jim'll Fix It*, two ABBA fans, Claire Lindeman and Clare Doggett, got the opportunity to meet their idols and see them at work at London's CBS recording studios.

Agnetha during the *Jim'll Fix It* programme.

On 4 January, the four Swedes flew to New York to take part in a UNICEF gala which showcased ten of the biggest pop acts in the world. Among the artists were the Bee Gees, Olivia Newton-John, Rod Stewart, John Denver and Donna Summer. As well as refusing any payment, each of the performers donated the royalties from one song to UNICEF. ABBA had decided to give 'Chiquitita' its worldwide première and this gala was obviously an excellent platform for the new song but, curiously, Atlantic didn't release the single in the USA until the end of the year.

THE MUSIC FOR UNICEF CONCERT
A GIFT OF SONG

1979

'We all know that there is no happy divorce. The reason behind our separation is one of those things I definitely don't want to go into.' AGNETHA

Although Björn and Agnetha had decided to separate a few months earlier, they officially announced their divorce at the beginning of January. The couple said that ABBA were not going to break up but, despite Björn and Agnetha's declarations, the press continued to speculate on the reasons for their separation and the future of the group.

Agnetha — who hadn't written a song for four years — had specially composed a new track for her forthcoming compilation album, *Tio År Med Agnetha* (Ten Years With Agnetha), which CBS-Cupol were going to release throughout Scandinavia.

'The fact that I was chosen came as a surprise to me. I've wanted to try something new outside ABBA for a long time. Even though I only had a small role, the first day of filming was very tough.' FRIDA

At the beginning of February, Frida spent a few days in Seville, Spain, filming her début acting role in the new Stig Björkman full-length movie *Gå På Vattnet Om Du Kan* (Walk On Water If You Can).

Frida with Lena Nyman and director Stig Björkman.

The single 'Chiquitita", which had been re- leased mid-January, became a big hit in many countries. The song, a ballad with a slightly Latin-American feel, was very well received in Spain and in South America, so ABBA decided to record a Spanish version with lyrics written by Buddy and Mary McCluskey, who worked for RCA in Argentina. The Spanish 'Chiquitita' hit No. 1 and helped ABBA achieve a convin- cing breakthrough in South America.

As there was no Lasse Hallström-directed promo clip for 'Chiqui- tita', Stig and ABBA decided to use a sequence made for the BBC in Leysin. The performance, filmed outdoors in front of a snowman, became the official clip for the song — although one wonders why they choose a wintry and snowy atmosphere for a beautiful melody with a sunny Latin-American feel.

Mid-February, ABBA took off for Leysin, Switzerland, where they were to record the TV show *ABBA In Switzerland*, part of the *Snowtime Special* series produced by the BBC. During their stay, the four Swedes mixed business and pleasure, making the most of the snow on the ski slopes.

Agnetha Björn Benny

The *ABBA In Switzerland* show was filmed in a big top with an audience of 2000. Even though ABBA mimed to playback tapes, they were accompanied on stage by three musicians. The group performed some of their hits and previewed four tracks from their forthcoming album. *ABBA In Switzerland* was screened in a number of European countries over the Easter holidays.

On 8 March, the four members of ABBA and Stig and his wife Gudrun attended the annual dinner organised by King Carl Gustav at the Royal Palace of Stockholm. Among the 160 ministers, ambassadors and other distinguished guests present was the future Swedish Prime Minister, Olof Palme (sadly assassinated in February 1986).

MENU

Crème d'oseille
Suprême de sole Champs-Elysées
Gelinotte Lucullus
Roquefort à l'Armagnac
Sorbet aux fruits de la passion.

(Menu written in French, according to tradition.)

The *Voulez-Vous* album and the 'Does Your Mother Know' single were released simultaneously in many countries at the end of April. Although *Voulez-Vous* is an album with a disco feel, the famous ABBA sound is still recognisable. Björn and Benny just added a few disco ingredients to their arrangements.

'This ABBA album is real quality. Their music is sophisticated and quite complex and a lot of the tracks need to be heard a few times before you get hooked. If you listen to "Voulez-Vous" with the volume turned right up, you realise that it's an ideal disco track.'
Mats Olsson *(Expressen)*

'ABBA is a booming industry. The name sells the products — the products sell themselves. *Voulez-Vous*: ten songs, every one a winner, already two are big hits. ABBA aren't my cup of tea but I admire them for their consistency in combining quality with appeal. *Voulez-Vous* cannot fail.'
Steve Gett *(Melody Maker)*

The single 'Does Your Mother Know' proved, once again, that ABBA were always looking for new ideas for each song. The track was rockier than usual and, for the first time, Björn sang lead vocal on the A-side, with Agnetha and Frida on backing vocals.

Does Your Mother Know

The 'Voulez-Vous' and 'Does Your Mother Know' videos were filmed by Lasse Hallström at the Europa Films Studios in Stockholm. The director re-created a discotheque environment to reflect the dance beats of the songs.

On 3 May, the four Swedes took part in a demonstration in the centre of Stockholm, with more than 500 artists and musicians, to protest against the government's attempts to block the creation of an agency aimed at finding work especially for artists. At the end of this day of protest, a petition was sent to the Minister of Employment.

Mid-May, Agnetha, Björn, Benny and Anni-Frid began rehearsals at the Grünewaldsalen concert hall in Stockholm for the forthcoming tour. A few days later, they gave two surprise concerts at nightclubs in Landskrona and Norrköping, accompanied by their musicians.

'I haven't got good memories of this period because I had to work in a hurry. Since the album had a disco sound, we decided to take the photos inside the Alexandra discotheque in Stockholm. I then went to London to work on the artwork for the sleeve and to add some star effects and some brightness on the neon light.' RUNE SÖDERQVIST

ABBA   Voulez-Vous

'I was aware of the Serge Gainsbourg/Jane Birkin song "Je t'aime, moi non plus"; I expect there's a bit of "voulez-vous" in there somewhere . . . What I had in mind before I even had the title was a kind of a nightclub scene, with a certain amount of sexual tension and eyes looking at each other.' BJÖRN

Greetings
from Stockholm

At the end of May, ABBA went to Madrid to record two TV shows: *300 Millones* and *Aplauso*. Both programmes were televised in Spain and also in most Spanish-speaking countries.

Voulez-Vous/Angeleyes

After a break during the month of July, the four members of ABBA continued rehearsals for the forthcoming tour in August at the Europa Films Studios in Sundbyberg, near Stockholm.

Björn invited his new girlfriend, Lena Källersjö, to spend a few days with him in Los Angeles.

Between 13 September and 7 October, ABBA performed in eighteen North American cities. After a break, the group carried on with a series of concerts in Europe, between 19 October and 15 November.

'The four of us decided we had so much more to give, but it was strange in the studio. When I used to ask my wife to do things, suddenly she wasn't my wife. She was someone else.'
BJÖRN

Anni-Frid, on tour with ABBA, couldn't attend the Stockholm première of the film *Gå På Vattnet Om Du Kan* on 17 September.

GÅ PÅ VATTNET OM DU KAN

Det började som en kärlekshistoria...

LENA NYMAN · TOMAS PONTÉN
Claire Wikholm · Norman Briski · Annifrid Lyngstad
Regi Stig Björkman efter manus av Sun Axelsson
Prod. Svenska Filminstitutet/Treklövern HB/Audiovision Investment · Färg · Distr. Europa Film

Estoy Soñando

GIMME! GIMME! GIMME!

The new single 'Gimme! Gimme! Gimme! (A Man After Midnight)' was released mid-October and became one of ABBA's biggest hits of 1979. Dominated by a forceful disco beat, it was the perfect track to promote the new compilation *Greatest Hits Vol. 2*.

ABBA Greatest Hits Vol. 2

On 4 November, Agnetha made a dramatic return to the *Svensktoppen* chart with 'När Du Tar Mig I Din Famn'. The song, which was included on her compilation album *Tio År Med Agnetha*, became her fourth No. 1 hit in Sweden.

The single 'I Have A Dream' was a perfect way to end an incredibly successful decade for ABBA. While the single climbed the charts, the four Swedes were awarded numerous gold and platinum discs for their previous singles and albums.

Although ABBA's image of 'two happy couples' had been tarnished by a divorce, they were now considered superstars. The new edition of the *Guinness Book Of Records* said, 'The group has sold the most records in the history of music after the Beatles.' Sales had been estimated at 150 million in only six years.

'What gives us the most pleasure is that we have proved music can come from anywhere, not just England or North America.' STIG ANDERSON

I HAVE A DREAM

In September 1979, ABBA started the most important tour of their career, with a schedule of 41 concerts in North America and the main countries of Europe (including six nights at London's Wembley Arena). Although they didn't like touring, the adventure was marked by excitement and anticipation. The concert programme consisted of 25 songs without an interval, accompanied by their most loyal session musicians. The tour involved 50 people, 40-50 tons of equipment and two buses for the musicians and technicians. To make travelling easier in North America, the group hired a Learjet. Visually, the set design was centred on a Nordic theme combining shades of blue, white and purple. Stage designer Rune Söderqvist worked in close collaboration with costume designers Owe Sandström and Lars Wigenius. Rune's blue-and-white mountains on the backdrop would later become Polar Music's official logo. ABBA's triumphant journey across two continents was vividly captured on film by Swedish director Urban Lasson in the television special *ABBA In Concert*.

Rehearsals began in May 1979 at Grünewaldshallen concert hall in Stockholm, and continued between 1 and 27 August at the Europa Films Studios in Sundbyberg. One of the big surprises on the tour was 'I Have A Dream' which would feature a different children's choir in each town. Another was 'I'm Still Alive', a song written and performed by Agnetha on the piano, as well as 'The Way Old Friends Do', a very emotional farewell hymn, with Benny playing the accordion.

Dress rehearsal.

Reporters from US newspapers and magazines visited the tour rehearsals at the Europa Films studios in August.

ABBA Live

Press conference in Edmonton.

Edmonton
Vancouver
Seattle
Portland
Concord
Anaheim
San Diego
Tempe
Las Vegas
Omaha
St Paul
Milwaukee
Chicago
New York
Boston
Washington DC
Montreal
Toronto
Gothenburg
Stockholm
Copenhagen
Paris
Rotterdam
Dortmund
Munich
Zurich
Vienna
Stuttgart
Bremen
Frankfurt
Brussels
London
Stafford
Glasgow
Dublin

191

North American & European Tour 1979

ABBA

Kodachrome TRANSPARENCY

PROCESSED BY KODAK

Meeting with Swedish Ambassador to the USA Wilhelm Wachtmeister and his wife Ulla.

Kodachrome TRANSPARENCY

PROCESSED BY KODAK

RELAXING

ABBA

Agnetha with Burt Ward, who played 'Robin' in the Batman TV series.

ABBA

Party after the Los Angeles concert.

'I certainly didn't look upon us as a live band.
It was nice to meet the fans, meet the audience.
But it took away the time creating new songs.
Because writing on the road didn't work for us.'
BJÖRN

'It was like a great party all the time. The crew was so big. It was very different compared
to rock groups. This was like a real family, young and older people all together.'
MATS RONANDER, guitarist

AFTONBLADET

ABBA : les chauds suédois

OH, ABBA!

FIRST NIGHT SPECIAL

What a damp squib for Bonfire Night

Succé för ABBA

ROCK POLISH, BUT NO PASSION

The love and loneliness of Abba stars

Abba : une musique sans frontiè

Abba en Belgique

Des centaines de fleurs pour accueillir les quatre stars suédoises

ABBA GRANDE PREMIER EN FRANCE!

'Rune Söderqvist and I came up with a colour scheme in white, blue and purple, which was meant to reflect the "chilly" Nordic origins of ABBA. We used the last three colours of the rainbow — blue, indigo and violet — as the starting point of our designs.' OWE SANDSTRÖM

Tomas Ledin arrived from Stockholm after having won the *Melodifestivalen 80* with his song 'Just Nu'.

After a break of a few months, ABBA returned to the stage in March 1980 for a series of concerts in Japan. They used the same team as they had for the 1979 tour. The only changes were that backing singer Birgitta Wollgård was replaced by Lena Eriksson and that parts of 'I Have A Dream' were sung in Japanese by the children's choir. ABBA gave eleven concerts (including six at the Tokyo Budokan) and were seen by more than 100,000 people. ABBA's tour in Japan was to be their very last tour.

Tokyo
Koriyama
Fukuoka
Osaka
Nagoya

A new decade began with new projects and, one could say, a 'new ABBA'. Their style was progressing more quickly than before and their lyrics reflect this evolution and maturity.

Björn and Benny, who were lacking inspiration, went on a working holiday to Barbados in January, an excursion which produced fine results as they came back with no less than five songs for the next album. Meanwhile, Agnetha and Frida, who had remained in Stockholm, began recording Spanish versions of several ABBA hits with the help of Michael B. Tretow and Sweden-based Spanish journalist Ana Martinez del Valle, who helped out with the pronunciation.

Frida with Ingemar Stenmark.

7 February — A reception was held at the Polar Music Studios to celebrate skiing champion Ingemar Stenmark's departure for the Winter Olympic Games in Lake Placid, USA. The party continued at the Shazam nightclub with the launch of a special LP entitled *Guldskivan OS 80*.

After a week of rehearsals, ABBA took off for Tokyo in order to start their Japanese tour: a series of eleven sell-out shows which confirmed ABBA's huge popularity in Japan.

Interview for the Austrian television programme *Okay*.

The Spanish ABBA album was released in May under the title *Gracias Por La Musica*. For the occasion a Spanish television crew came to Stockholm to film the show *Aplauso*. *Gracias Por La Musica* was an immense seller in the Hispanic-speaking world, reaching the Top 5 in both Spain and Argentina.

Agnetha was accompanied by her new boyfriend Dick Håkansson.

On 19 May, Görel Johnsen married Anders Hanser. The four Swedes attended the ceremony which took place in the chapel of Ulriksdal Castle, near Stockholm.

'I'm really fond of "The Winner Takes It All".
I remember the lyrics came in about two hours, which was really unusually quick.'
BJÖRN

On 12 July, the members of ABBA joined director Lasse Hallström in Marstrand, an island off the west coast of Sweden, to film the video for the forthcoming single 'The Winner Takes It All'.
The song was to become one of ABBA's biggest worldwide hits.

THE WINNER TAKES IT ALL

On 8 August, Björn, Benny and Frida flew to London to attend Pink Floyd's *The Wall* concert and to promote their new single. They met the press, had an interview on Radio One and did some shopping on South Molton Street.

Björn, who's a jogging fanatic, trains in every town he visits.

Bilagan

Unika bilder
ABBA-STUDION
INIFRÅN

Så skapades den nya skivan
–Björn och Agnetha berättar

Söndag 9 november 1980

Recording sessions for the *Super Trouper* album continued at the Polar Music Studios until mid-October.

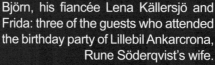

On 23 August, Björn took part in th Stockholm Marathon. He passe the finishing line after three hour and 22 minutes.

'The way people think of us has a lot to do with their imaginations and very little to do with us as people. They just see the surface, they don't have any in-depth view of us as people. They see only the bright side, the way we dress, the way we act.' FRIDA

At the end of August, Frida started a French course at the Norra Real training college for adults.

Björn, his fiancée Lena Källersjö and Frida: three of the guests who attended the birthday party of Lillebil Ankarcrona, Rune Söderqvist's wife.

Photo shoot on the avenue Foch.

On 21 October, ABBA arrived in Paris for two days of promotion. The high point of their visit was the recording of the television show *Stars*. They also met journalists at the George V Hotel.

TV rehearsals at the Pavillon Baltard in Nogent.

Frida, Agnetha and Björn with Alain Boublil.

ABBA performed 'The Winner Takes It All' and 'Super Trouper'.

On the evening of 3 October, all the group's friends and work colleagues gathered in the Europa Films Studios, where the photos for the sleeve of the new album were to be taken, as well as some footage for the 'Super Trouper' and 'Happy New Year' promotional films. To create a circus atmosphere in the large studio, Rune Söderqvist called in Swede François Bronett, who was a professional in this field. He arrived with about twenty performers including clowns, jugglers, acrobats and fire-eaters. He also brought along two white horses, a donkey and two poodles. Several photographers were invited to take photos of the event. Lasse Hallström completed filming of the promo clips on 4, 5 and 8 October.

'Actually, the picture should have been taken at Piccadilly Circus, but the English authorities didn't think it was such a good idea to have a lot of animals and people in costume standing around down there.'
FRIDA

'It's the first time that I've directed one of the world's biggest pop groups and an entire circus . . . at the same time!'
RUNE SÖDERQVIST

Making the album sleeve

'The Super Trouper is a spotlight.
The largest and most powerful of all
the spotlights you'll see at a concert . . .
shining like the sun.'
BJÖRN

15 November — Benny, Frida, Björn and Lena Källersjö attended Rod Stewart's concert at the Isstadion in Stockholm.

On 27 November, ABBA appeared on the German TV programm Show Express. As their promotional trip to Germany had bee cancelled following a kidnap threat, it was decided that the fou Swedes would stay in Stockholm. ABBA performed three song and were interviewed by host Michael Schanze via a live satellit link-up segment from one of the Swedish Television studios.

Super Trouper, which was first released in Sweden on 3 November, became one of ABBA's bestselling albums ever. Widely regarded as one of the group's finest records, it contains a brilliant selection of songs including the dance track 'Lay All Your Love On Me' and 'The Way All Friends Do', a song recorded live at Wembley Arena in November 1979.

'For unlike some of their contemporaries in the mass market place (like, say, Wings and Supertramp), ABBA write great pop songs that have magic — that ethereal quality which no critic can define, analyse or rationalise. "The Winner Takes It All", included here, is perhaps the supreme example of this magical ambiance. Unusually for ABBA the lyrics have personal cutting power (presumably a reference to the split between Agnetha and Björn).'
Lynden Barber *(Melody Maker)*

'They possess a chilly magic. In terms of producing straightforward pop they are almost unbeatable.'
James Johnson *(London Evening Standard)*

Following the *Show Express* programme, the group recorded a special version of their song 'Happy New Year', standing around a white piano with candelabra and champagne — a sequence which would regularly air on television in many countries.

Mireille Mathieu
Bravo tu as gagné

ns chanter
ur le Bon Dieu

In December, Benny began production on Norwegian singer Finn Kalvik's second album *Natt Og Dag*. A few days later, he and Björn produced 'Bravo Tu As Gagné', Mireille Mathieu's French version of 'The Winner Takes It All'. The song was recorded at the Polar Music Studios, where Frida joined them on background vocals.

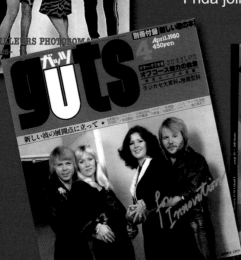

VECKO
Revyn

AGNETHA FÄLTSKOGS
SVÅRA LIV PÅ TOPPEN
JÄTTELIKT SKOL-START-EXTRA
28 sidor med allt för dej som
pluggar i höst

Look-in

ABBA

SCHLAGER

KEITH RICHARD

ABBA BIT FÖR BIT

6 January — Björn married Lena Källersjö in the strictest privacy, with only twelve people present. The ceremony took place in a little church at Grythyttan, in the Swedish province of Västmanland. Nobody knew about the wedding except for the couple's families. There were no photographers or journalists present, and it was a complete contrast to the hustle surrounding Björn's marriage to Agnetha in 1971.

24 January — a TV crew filmed ABBA on stage at the Berns Theatre. The group, dressed up in their Brighton stage clothes, performed 'Hovas Vittne', a tribute song to Stig with humorous lyrics, written by Björn, Benny, Michael B. Tretow and Rune Söderqvist — 200 copies were pressed in red vinyl.

25 January 1981 was a memorable day as Stig celebrated his fiftieth birthday at his magnificent mansion on the island of Djurgården in Stockholm. The party began at seven o'clock in the morning when Björn and Benny climbed into his bedroom via a fire-escape ladder and began playing 'Happy Birthday Stig' on the accordion while humming along. They had just finished when a seven-woman choir (among them were Frida, Agnetha, Görel and Lena Ulvaeus) entered the room to serenade him with a birthday song. An enormous buffet was waiting in the lounge later and an orchestra of fifteen musicians welcomed guests as they arrived. More than 400 people came to pay homage to the king of Swedish showbusiness. After dinner, which was exclusively for Stig's close friends and family, there was a video shown on a massive screen. The guests had the opportunity to relive the best moments of the day, which had been filmed by a TV crew, and to see ABBA singing 'Hovas Vittne'. As a grand finale, fireworks lit up the sky, spelling out the words 'Long Live Stikkan!'. A few days later, Stig thanked his friends through a mini-newspaper entitled *Stikkan Expressen*.

1981

On 12 February, Anni-Frid and Benny announced that they would be filing for divorce. Polar Music made no comment on the matter apart from a bulletin saying, 'Benny Andersson and Anni-Frid Lyngstad have decided to separate. On a business level, the decision has nothing at all to do with ABBA's work.' The couple refused to give any comments but the newspapers speculated and revealed the main reason for the divorce: Benny had fallen for a 37-year-old TV reporter called Mona Nörklit who was, in fact, Rune Söderqvist's sister-in-law. The effect on the group was not instant, but how could the world-dominating quartet continue after yet another body blow?

Agnetha was chosen as the figurehead for an anti-tobacco campaign in Sweden. A strange choice as she was a heavy smoker!

26 May — a two-week exhibition of ABBA's costumes was launched by the Together Gallery in Stockholm.

Agnetha and Ingela Forsman were invited to write a song for the *Melodifestivalen*. The song, performed by Kicki Moberg, was 'Men Natten Är Vår'. On the B-side was 'Här Är Mitt Liv', another of Agnetha's compositions performed in English as 'I'm Still Alive' during ABBA's 1979-80 Tour. Kicki finished in fifth place in the *Melodifestivalen*.

In April, American TV presenter Dick Cavett came to Stockholm to record the *Dick Cavett Meets ABBA* show. The programme, produced by Swedish Television, consisted of an interview with the four Swedes and a live concert in front of a television studio audience.

Björn and Lena travelled to the Hockenheim racing circuit in Germany to give Swedish driver Tommy 'Slim' Borgudd some encouragement before the Formula 1 Grand Prix. Tommy's car had been sponsored by ABBA.

An award from the German magazine *Pop Rocky*.

Recording sessions for the next album continued. Björn admitted that, from now on, the private lives of the four ABBA members would be a source of inspiration for their lyrics.

Frida and Claes af Geijerstam were invited to present *Lite Grand I Örat*, a series of four shows for Swedish Television in which they also sang along with other guests. The rehearsals and filming of the shows took place during the second half of August at the Grand Hotel in Stockholm.

'Let The Sun Shine In' — Peter Lundblad, Frida and Kicki Danielsso

Agnetha with Barbara Dickson.

12 September — ABBA travelled to Bournemouth, England, for the CBS Sales conference. The members of the sales team were very touched by the group's presence at their annual meeting, as they very rarely had the chance to meet the artists they worked for during the year. The four Swedes had also the chance to meet Jaap Eggermont, the creator of the *Stars On 45* concept, who had had a big hit that year with his 'ABBA Medley'.

The Polar Music offices moved to a new building located at Hamngatan 11, in the very centre of Stockholm.

In December, Polar Music finally released the Christmas album recorded by Agnetha and her daughter Linda a year earlier.

'When you've gone through a separation, like all of us had done at the time, it puts a certain mood on the work. Perhaps there was a bit of sadness or bitterness that coloured the making of The Visitors album.' FRIDA

The end of the year brought a new single 'One Of Us', which was taken from the new (and last) studio LP *The Visitors*, released around the same time. The single would become the group's final major worldwide hit and the album stormed up the charts almost everywhere. The songs on the album indicated that Björn and Benny were adopting a different and more mature approach to their songwriting activities. 'I Let The Music Speak', a track on *The Visitors*, seemed to underline their ambitions for the future as it was structured like a theatrical number. Björn and Benny had always wanted to write a musical — a dream which was about to become reality. In December, they had a meeting in Stockholm with Britain's most successful lyricist Tim Rice to discuss a potential collaboration.

Outside view of the studio.

'I immediately thought of this place when I found out that one of the songs was called "Like An Angel Passing Through My Room". Julius Kronberg had painted this huge angel, called Eros, which you can see on the sleeve.' RUNE SÖDERQVIST

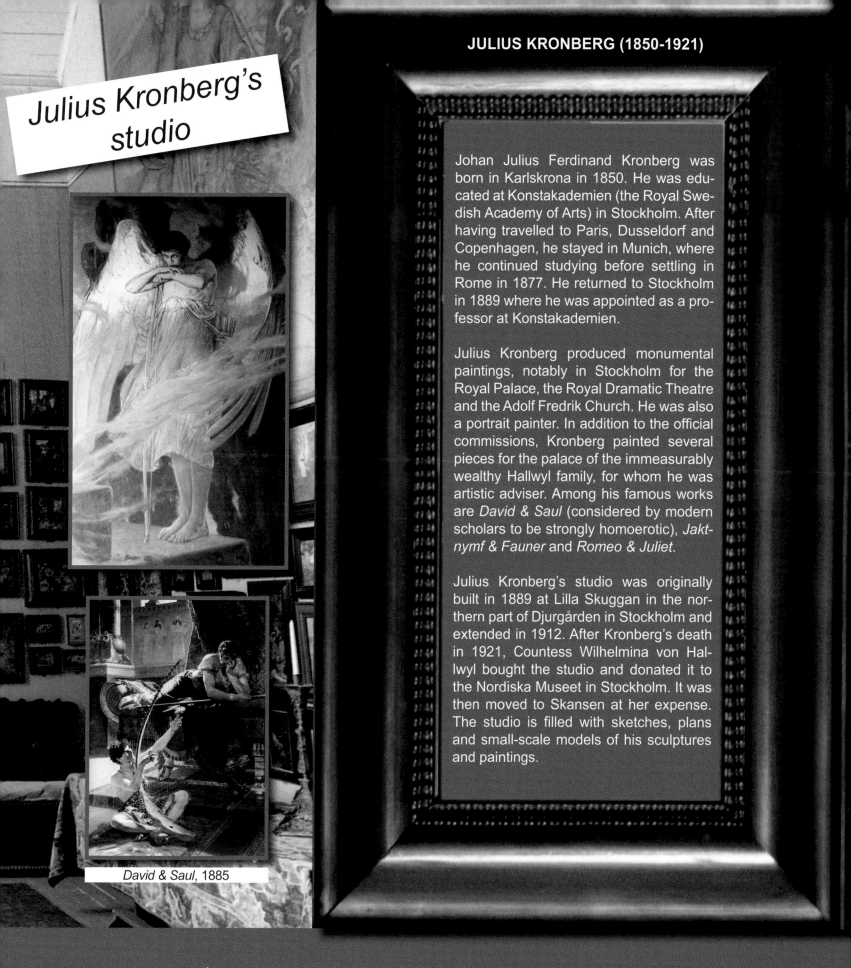

Julius Kronberg's studio

JULIUS KRONBERG (1850-1921)

Johan Julius Ferdinand Kronberg was born in Karlskrona in 1850. He was educated at Konstakademien (the Royal Swedish Academy of Arts) in Stockholm. After having travelled to Paris, Dusseldorf and Copenhagen, he stayed in Munich, where he continued studying before settling in Rome in 1877. He returned to Stockholm in 1889 where he was appointed as a professor at Konstakademien.

Julius Kronberg produced monumental paintings, notably in Stockholm for the Royal Palace, the Royal Dramatic Theatre and the Adolf Fredrik Church. He was also a portrait painter. In addition to the official commissions, Kronberg painted several pieces for the palace of the immeasurably wealthy Hallwyl family, for whom he was artistic adviser. Among his famous works are *David & Saul* (considered by modern scholars to be strongly homoerotic), *Jaktnymf & Fauner* and *Romeo & Juliet*.

Julius Kronberg's studio was originally built in 1889 at Lilla Skuggan in the northern part of Djurgården in Stockholm and extended in 1912. After Kronberg's death in 1921, Countess Wilhelmina von Hallwyl bought the studio and donated it to the Nordiska Museet in Stockholm. It was then moved to Skansen at her expense. The studio is filled with sketches, plans and small-scale models of his sculptures and paintings.

David & Saul, 1885

'The sleeve designer was a close friend who saw what had happened in our lives. The picture really reflects what was happening. Basically, we'd had enough!' BJÖRN

On 3 January, Lena Ulvaeus gave birth to a baby daughter called Emma. A week later, on 10 January, Benny and Mona, who got married five weeks before in a simple ceremony, celebrated the birth of their son Ludvig.

Head Over Heels

On 15 February, Frida began recording her first solo album in the English language. The ABBA singer, who had been captivated by Phil Collins's album *Face Value*, had asked him to produce the record. The Polar Music Studios were booked for six weeks and Phil brought his own musicians and engineer to Stockholm. With the exception of 'You Know What I Mean' (previously recorded by Collins on *Face Value*), all the songs had been written especially for the project. A British TV crew, directed by Stuart Orme, filmed a one-hour documentary entitled *Something's Going On — The Making of An Album*.

During the first months of 1982, Björn and Benny reduced their musical activities considerably in order to be able to spend more time at home with their families. Due to a lack of energy and creativity, the plans to make an altogether new ABBA album were completely discarded. Instead, the two musicians decided to release a double album anthology of ABBA's singles including two new tracks. In April, new songwriting sessions had been started that eventually produced three new tracks: 'You Owe Me One', 'Just Like That' and 'I Am The City'. After the usual holiday in July, Björn and Benny were back in the studio in August to complete the very last ABBA songs: 'Cassandra', 'Under Attack' and 'The Day Before You Came'.

1982

In August, Agnetha made her début as a movie actress in a film entitled *Raskenstam*, directed by Swedish actor Gunnar Hellström, who also played the title role. Agnetha played the part of Lisa Mattsson, a fisherman's daughter, who falls madly in love with Gustav Raskenstam and has two children by him. The film retraces the true story of the Swedish Don Juan who swindled several hundred women in the 1940s by seducing them and promising them marriage. *Raskenstam* was released in August 1983.

'When I read the script for Raskenstam, I knew that I would be able to play Lisa and it was fantastic to make the movie. I have seldom felt as satisfied as I did then. I think that most of it had to do with that I wasn't myself, I was somebody else!' AGNETHA

Agnetha, who had just finished recording a duet with Tomas Ledin, entitled 'Never Again', announced that she was going to record a solo album the following year. The name of the producer, Mike Chapman, would be revealed later. The single 'Never Again' was released at the end of September and reached No. 2 in the Swedish charts.

In November, ABBA started their promotional campaign for the new single 'The Day Before You Came' and the compilation album *The Singles — The First Ten Years* with a three-day visit to the UK. During their stay in London, they met the press, gave interviews and appeared on the TV programmes *Saturday Superstore* and *The Late, Late Breakfast Show*. At a reception organised by Epic at the Belfry Club to celebrate the group's ten years together, they were presented with 23 gold discs in an enormous frame.

'"The Day Before You Came" was something that was completely misunderstood by the public. Or it was too early, or something like that. It was so different from anything we'd done. We might have continued for a while longer if that had been No. 1. But since it wasn't, we felt "This is the time!"' BJÖRN

The double anniversary album *The Singles — The First Ten Years* featured 21 of ABBA's most popular singles released from 1972 to 1982, plus the two new tracks 'The Day Before You Came' and 'Under Attack'. The compilation was an immediate success and sold extremely well.

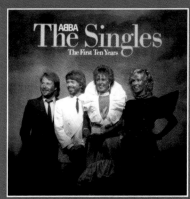

Frida's long-awaited solo LP was released in September, preceded by the single 'I Know There's Something Going On'. It was her first album since the *Frida Ensam* project and the first to be given worldwide release. Frida was very proud of the album. It had been a new experience for her and it was clear that she wanted to create something that was a radical departure from ABBA.

Something's Going On includes contributions from songwriting talents such as Russ Ballard, Bryan Ferry, Stephen Bishop, Per Gessle, Giorgio Moroder, Jim Rafferty, Tomas Ledin and Phil Collins himself. It also featured 'Here We'll Stay', a duet by Phil and Frida. The record was ambitious and very risky, but Frida's collaboration with Phil Collins proved to be extremely successful and the album sold one and a half million copies and the single three million copies worldwide.

'When it came up that I was going to do a solo album my first thought was to have Phil Collins as my producer. I liked his album Face Value so much — I must have listened to it almost every day for eight months. Without Phil I wouldn't have gone ahead — I wanted him that much!'
FRIDA

Between 7 September and 3 November, Frida went on a promotional trip with Görel Hanser. They visited the United States, Canada, and several European countries.

Frida goes solo

ABBA star Frida goes on her own

IN THE last couple of years, ABBA Frida Lyngstad has turned her life upside down.

She's been divorced from fellow ABBA mem...

Frida's Solo-LP Something's Going On

PRODUCED BY PHIL COLLINS
Assisted by Hugh Padgham

Frida Something's Going On

BRAVO
Bronzene Siegerin
der Otto-Wahl 1982
FRIDA

INVITATION
POUR 1 PERSONNE

La Société Nationale de Télévision en couleur
Antenne 2
vous prie de lui faire l'honneur d'assister à l'émission publique

Champs-Élysées
présentée par Michel Drucker

diffusée en direct

ENREGT LE — 6 OCT. 1982 — à 20 heures 30

Fermeture des portes à 20 heures

ESPACE CARDIN
1, Avenue Gabriel
75008 PARIS

1982 nr.12

POP FOTO

tweede liefde
BENNY NEYMAN

SUPERPRIJSVRAAG
van Frida **50 kerstkado**'s voor jou

DOE MAAR

Following their British visit, the four Swedes flew to Germany on 8 November. They appeared on *Tommy's Pop Show* but their most spectacular TV appearance was on the *Show Express* where they performed three songs before a live audience.

19 November — ABBA took part in the programme *Nöjesmaskinen* on Swedish TV. They were interviewed by Stina Lundberg and Sven Melander in a relaxed atmosphere. Between video clips, they all joked and talked about their work, the past and their projects. They closed the show by singing a verse and the chorus of 'Thank You For The Music' accompanied by piano and guitar, and 'Under Attack' performed to playback.

At a private reception on the top floor of Polar Music, Stig handed out a number of awards for record sales in Sweden. Each member of ABBA, as well as Michael B. Tretow, were given a gold disc for *The Visitors* album. Agnetha and Tomas Ledin were presented with a gold disc for 'Never Again' and Frida with a platinum disc for the *Something's Going On* album and a gold disc for the single.

11 December — ABBA appeared on Noel Edmonds's *Late, Late Breakfast Show* in Britain via a live link from a TV studio in Stockholm. Although no one knew it at the time, this was to be the last ever public performance by ABBA as a group.

ABBA had now been active for a decade and became the biggest group of the 1970s, with sales of approximately 200 million units. Although sessions for a new album took place in 1982, it appears that 'The Day Before You Came' was the very last ABBA recording. ABBA never officially broke up, but their four members were now concentrating on new individual projects and solo careers.

Although the capital of Sweden has changed since the 1970s, one is still able to see and visit ABBA-related sights when on holiday in Stockholm. Here's a selection of places in and outside the city where ABBA records, photos, films and promo clips were made.

Stortorget, in the heart of the Old Town (Gamla Stan).

Riddarholmen, in front of the City Hall.

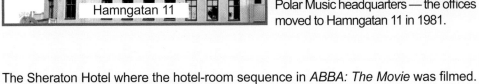

Hamngatan 11

Baldersgatan 1

Polar Music headquarters — the offices moved to Hamngatan 11 in 1981.

The Sheraton Hotel where the hotel-room sequence in *ABBA: The Movie* was filmed. The photo for *ABBA: The Album* was taken on the hotel roof in June 1977.

Tegelbacken 6

Sankt Eriksgatan 58-60

The Polar Music Studios closed in May 2004.

ABBA & THE CITY

An ABBA fan's guide to Stockholm.

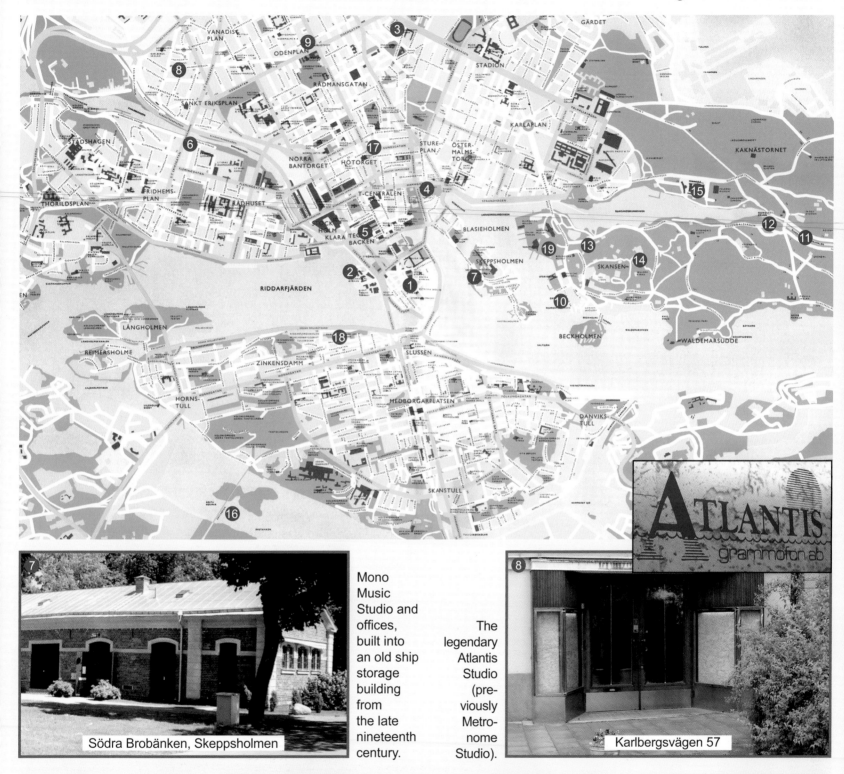

Mono Music Studio and offices, built into an old ship storage building from the late nineteenth century.

Södra Brobänken, Skeppsholmen

The legendary Atlantis Studio (previously Metronome Studio).

Karlbergsvägen 57

Hard Rock Cafe Stockholm, Sveavägen 75.

Gröna Lund amusement park — ABBA performed here on 30 June 1975.

The Ferris wheel was sold in India and replaced by a small roller coaster in 2007.

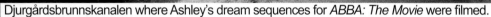

Djurgårdsbrunnskanalen where Ashley's dream sequences for *ABBA: The Movie* were filmed.

Hootenanny Singers and ABBA (in 1970) had photo sessions under this rain shelter.

The Ulla Winbladh inn, Rosendalsvägen 8 — ABBA had two well-known photo sessions here in 1975 and 1976.

At the Skansen open-air museum, don't forget to visit the famous Julius Kronberg Studio and see the Dala horse located on Orsakullen.

Sjöhistoriska Museet (National Maritime Museum), Djurgårdsbrunnsvägen 24.

Årstabron (a view from Liljeholmsbron), the bridge seen in 'The Day Before You Came' promo film.

Stairs in the 'Head Over Heels' promo film — located at the corner of Kungsgatan and Malmskillnadsgatan.

This house, located on Bastugatan, was used on the cover of Agnetha's *Elva Kvinnor i Ett Hus* LP.

Stig Anderson's grave in the Galärkyrkogården cemetery.

Gripsholms Slott (castle) — 50 km (31 miles) west of Stockholm.

Photo sessions and sequences for *ABBA: The Movie* and the National TV commercials were filmed in the Palace gardens.

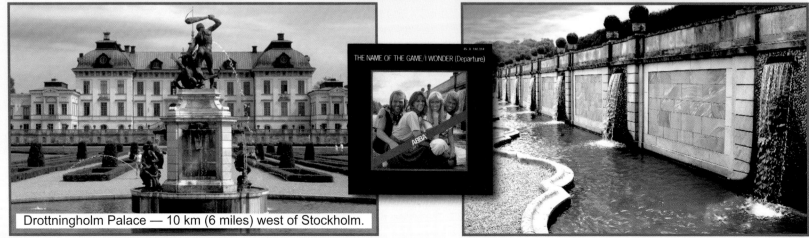
Drottningholm Palace — 10 km (6 miles) west of Stockholm.

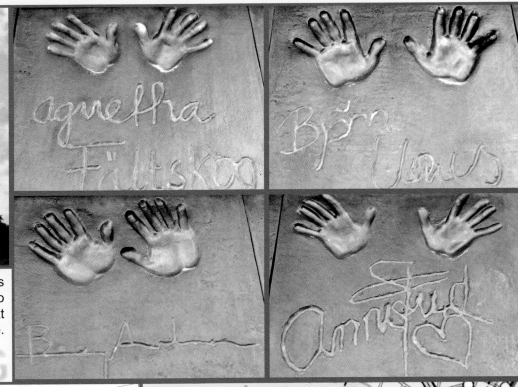

Liseberg amusement park — see ABBA's handprints in bronze (made on 29 January 1977). ABBA also have their star in the pavement outside the park, next to the main entrance.

GÖTEBORG

Göteborg's Scandinavium concert hall where ABBA performed in 1977 and 1979. *Jesus Christ Superstar* (with Agnetha) played there in 1972.

The island of Marstrand, on the west coast of Sweden, where Lasse Hallström directed ABBA in 'The Winner Takes It All' promo film.

The restaurant and conference hall *Societetshuset*.

After three solo albums, *Wrap Your Arms Around Me*, *Eyes Of A Woman*, *I Stand Alone*, and *Kom Följ Med i Vår Karusell,* a children's album with her son Christian, Agnetha withdrew completely from showbusiness.

In 1990, she married surgeon Tomas Sonnenfeld but they divorced two years later. Far from the public gaze in her big house in Ekerö, near Stockholm, she has been called 'the new Greta Garbo'.

In 1996, with the help of her journalist friend Brita Åhman, she published a memoir, *Som Jag Är*. Translated into English under the title *As I Am — ABBA Before & Beyond*, it was interesting mainly for the photographs it contained. The publication of this semi-autobiography and the simultaneous release of a compilation of Agnetha's songs, entitled *My Love My Life*, suggested that Agnetha was on the brink of making a comeback. But this was not to be the case until 2004, when after seventeen years of silence, she returned to the musical spotlight with a new album entitled *My Colouring Book*, featuring thirteen covers which can be considered to be a personal tribute to her past musical influences. Agnetha is not comfortable before the media, but she agreed to give some interviews for Swedish television for the promotion of her new album.

She also hit the headlines that same year for not turning up at the *Mamma Mia!*'s fifth birthday celebrations in London on 6 April — a date which also marked the thirtieth anniversary of ABBA's victory in Brighton. Agnetha's absence was a big disappointment for both her fans and her ex-ABBA colleagues.

After this comeback, Agnetha's public appearances have been more frequent in Sweden, although she seems to be back in the shadows again. Time will tell if plans for a new solo album are rumour or reality.

AGNETHA

After ABBA

Since 1966, Björn's collaboration with Benny Andersson has been almost constant. In 1984, they wrote a musical with Tim Rice entitled *Chess*. The stage show ran for almost three years in the West End of London but did not achieve the same success on Broadway. After having worked with numerous Swedish artists (including Gemini and Josefin Nilsson), Björn and Benny began working on what is considered to be their masterpiece: *Kristina Från Duvemåla*, a musical based on *Utvandrarna* (The Emigrants), a tetralogy by Swedish novelist Vilhelm Moberg. The musical ran for some years in Sweden and an English version is apparently in preparation.

In 1999, Björn was back in the spotlight, thanks to his close collaboration in the smash-hit musical *Mamma Mia!*, based on the songs of ABBA.

Benny has been passionate about folk music since childhood. He writes new songs and produces new talent on his Mono Music label, and even joins folk musicians on stage at concerts. He has released two solo albums and has recorded three albums with his own band, BAO (Benny Anderssons Orkester), with whom he plays select concerts in Sweden and abroad.

His other passions include race horses (of which he owns several) and collecting works of art at auction in the company of his wife Mona.

The success of *Kristina Från Duvemåla* has surpassed all expectations and made him one of the most respected composers in Sweden. At the end of 1997, he was chosen to be one of the six members of the committee which runs the Stockholm Royal Opera.

Although Benny felt he'd had just about enough of the ABBA revival, he has on several occasions performed old ABBA songs on stage, with or without his BAO band.

Nowadays, Benny Andersson and Björn Ulvaeus are frequently at premières of the musical *Mamma Mia!*, every now and then joined by Frida. At the show's fifth anniversary in London, they were presented with a very special award for achieving record sales of 360 million worldwide in 30 years.

CHESS

TIM RICE

BJÖRN ULVAEUS

KRISTINA 15c

FRÅN DUVEMÅLA

TAYLORS
JUN 25
1860
MINN.

✿ BENNY ANDERSSONS ORKESTER ✿
MED HELEN SJÖHOLM

BAO!

ANNI-FRID

In 1983 Frida took part in the French children's TV musical *Abbacadabra*, for which she recorded the duet 'Belle' with French singer Daniel Balavoine, and its English version 'Time' with B.A. Robertson. She released a second solo album, *Shine*, in 1984 and also made occasional contributions to other artists' records such as Adam Ant or the Swedish duo Ratata.

Frida then chose to retire from the music scene in order to devote all of her time to her new passion: the environment. In 1992, she released the single 'Saltwater' to raise funds for her *Artister För Miljö — Det Naturliga Steget* association and returned to the stage for a one-off concert with other artists at the Royal Palace of Stockholm. She did not feel out of place in this setting — she has been a great friend of Queen Silvia's for many years and she married Prince Ruzzo Reuss von Plauen, a childhood friend of King Carl XVI Gustaf.

In 1996, Frida made a dazzling return to the music scene with the excellent Swedish-language album *Djupa Andetag*. It was an enormous success, reaching No. 1 in the Swedish chart, but the album's release was limited to Scandinavia.

The late 1990s were a difficult time for Frida — her daughter Lise-Lotte was killed in a car accident and her husband Ruzzo died after a long illness.

In 2004, she recorded a song called 'The Sun Will Shine Again', written and produced by her long-time friend and former Deep Purple member Jon Lord, for which she did some promotion in Germany.

Nowadays, Frida lives a fairly low-profile life but every now and then appears at a party or charity function. Although she regularly attends premières of the musical *Mamma Mia!*, the hectic ABBA years no longer suit her, as she wants to retain the balance and harmony she has managed to acquire in her life over the past few years.

While attending the *Mamma Mia!* première in Berlin, in November 2007, she reported that she was planning to record demos with Jon Lord in order to make a new solo album.

Bang-a-Boomerang!

The ABBA revival

Who would have believed in 1982 that ten years later the music of ABBA would undergo a revival and many of their hits become firmly established pop classics?

Who would have thought that the cinema would be paying homage to them in several films, or that the duo Erasure or indeed Madonna would be topping the charts with ABBA songs?

Who could have imagined that the refrains of the group's songs would give birth to a musical (playing worldwide in a multitude of different languages), which would then be turned into a film starring Meryl Streep?

Absolutely no one, and certainly not Agnetha, Björn, Benny and Anni-Frid! When they decided to take a break after ten years of intense activity together, they could not have imagined that a second, even longer (and in certain countries more spectacular) period of success awaited them. And all this without singing a single note or recording a new song!

After being almost forgotten during the 1980s, ABBA found themselves rocketing to the top of the charts in 1992 with their compilation CD *ABBA Gold* (25 million copies sold). This success has continued, thanks to a fanbase of millions who accord ABBA cult status, perhaps started by the gay community, for whom ABBA were icons and who took the song 'Dancing Queen' for their own.

As during the 90s, the new millennium vibrates to the beat of ABBA songs, with sales of their discs increasing all the time. With more than 360 million records and discs sold worldwide, ABBA are the biggest selling pop group after the Beatles.

Did the members of ABBA have a secret for making people feel so happy on hearing their music? Perhaps, and if there is one, it is definitely to be found in the freshness of their refrains, and in the magic and timelessness of their songs.

236

MAMMA MIA!

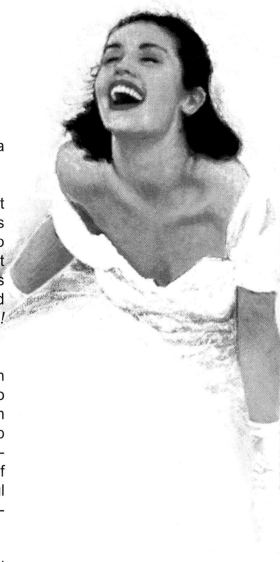

Although the title of the musical is taken from ABBA's 1975 chart-topper 'Mamma Mia', the plot has nothing to do with the story of the group itself:

Donna, a single mother and taverna keeper on a fictional Greek island, is about to marry off her daughter Sophie. Sophie has realised (by reading her mother's old diary) that one of three men is her father, so she secretly invites them to her wedding. All three show up, as do Tanya and Rosie, Donna's lifelong best friends, with whom she had a singing group called Donna and the Dynamos twenty years ago. Over 24 chaotic, magical hours, new love will bloom and old romances will be rekindled on this lush island full of possibilities . . . *Mamma Mia!* is a celebration of mothers and daughters, old friends and newfound family.

Mamma Mia! began in 1995 when producer Judy Craymer approached Björn and Benny with the project of a musical based on the songs of ABBA. The two Swedes were not totally convinced but did not close the door, saying, 'If you can find the right writer and story, well . . . let's see what happens . . .' The next step was when co-producer Richard East and Judy commissioned playwright Catherine Johnson to write a contemporary and romantic comedy around the hits of ABBA. The third woman behind what was to become one of the most successful musicals of all time was director Phyllida Lloyd, who had a background in theatre and opera.

Once Björn and Benny were finally convinced by the script, the production could start and the prestigious Prince Edward Theatre in London's West End was booked. The opening date of 6 April was chosen, just in time to celebrate the twenty-fifth anniversary of ABBA's victory in Brighton with 'Waterloo'.

The rest is history . . . While *Mamma Mia!* is still playing in London, Broadway and Las Vegas, and there are several productions playing simultaneously around the world. The musical has been seen by more than 30 million people in 160 cities around the world (in eight different languages) and has become a global entertainment phenomenon.

The film version of *Mamma Mia!*, starring Meryl Streep, Pierce Brosnan, Colin Firth, Stellan Skarsgård and Amanda Seyfried, was one of the box-office smashes of 2008.

With a prestigious cast, an incredible score, a wonderful screenplay and beautiful cinematography, the *Mamma Mia!* movie makes you want to pack your bags and head straight for a Greek island with ABBA playing on your iPod!

ACKNOWLEDGEMENTS

My heartfelt thanks go to my beloved Thierry for his support and enthusiasm throughout this project.

I particularly want to thank Bernd and Michael Scheiber for their friendship, their optimism and support at any time, Rod Campbell for his help, his advice and supervision of the texts and translations, Görel Hanser for being so helpful and for giving me access to ABBA's archives, Ingemar Bergman and Olle Rönnbäck at Polar Music and Rune Söderqvist.

Thank you to Sandra Wake at Plexus Publishing Ltd for having made *ABBA: The Scrapbook* a reality.

I would also like to thank: Vincent Astorri, Åsa Bergold (Polar Music), Alain Boublil, Denis Boursier, Lionel Brogi, David Charnley, Thérèse Chasseguet (Universal Music France), Ian Cole, Colin Collier, Gilles Colombani, Adam Davies, Bernard Deman, Annette Falck (IMS Bildbyrå), Lars Falck, Marc-André Francart, Nicolas Gayerie, Regina Grafunder, Gunilla Gunnerheim (Folkparkerna), Jeffrey de Hart, Catherine Hinard, Helga van de Kar, Ola Lager, Patrick Largeteau, Carsten Michael Laursen, Michael Leckebusch, David Legrand, Sten-Åke Magnusson, Benoît Manns, Philippe Michon, Jean-Claude Misse, Alex Mizrahi, Daniel Murgui-Tomas, Nora, Thomas Nordin, Jokke Norling, Tomas Nyh (EMA-Telstar), Jean Pajot, Carl Magnus Palm, Sven Åke Peterson (EMI Svenska AB), Lars Postner, Véronique Rapoport, Olle Rönnbäck (Polar Music), Marie-Laure Sanchez, Ron Spaulding, Christian de Tarlé (Universal Music France), Inger Svenneke, Laurence de Virville, Vogue France.

Thank you to Pär-Johan Goody Rohdin and Allan Goody for the translations of the Swedish press reviews.

Last but not least, thank you to Agnetha, Björn, Benny and Anni-Frid for their remarkable talent and for being a part of my life since 6 April 1974. I cannot forget Stig 'Stikkan' Anderson for having made Polar Music and ABBA's photographic archives available to me in the early 90s. Without his help this book wouldn't have been possible!

SOURCES

BOOKS
Mamma Mia! How Can I Resist You?, Benny Andersson, Björn Ulvaeus, Judy Craymer (Weidenfeld & Nicolson, 2006)
ABBA: Thank You For The Music, Carsten Michael Laursen (Lindhardt og Ringhof, 2002)
Bright Lights Dark Shadows: The Real Story of ABBA, Carl Magnus Palm (Omnibus Press, 2001)
As I Am — ABBA Before And Beyond, Agnetha Fältskog with Brita Åhman (Virgin, 1997)
ABBA: The Complete Recording Sessions, Carl Magnus Palm (Century 22, 1994)
ABBA Gold: The Complete Story, John Tobler (Century 22, 1993)
Stikkan: Den Börsnoterade Refrängsångaren, Oscar Hedlund (Sweden Music Förlag, 1983)
ABBA In Their Own Words, Rosemary York (Omnibus Press, 1982)
ABBA For The Record, John Tobler (Stafford Pemberton, 1980)
ABBA By ABBA, Christer Borg (Stafford Pemberton, 1977)

PRESS
International ABBA Magazine, ABBA 5 Years, Aftonbladet, Allers, Bravo, Bild Journalen, Dagens Nyheter, Das Freizeit Magazin, Expressen, France-Soir, Hemmets Journalen, Juke Box, La Dernière Heure, Le Soir, Podium, Poster, Record Mirror, Salut, Saxons, Se, Svensk Damtidning, Télérama, Vecko Revyn.

TELEVISION & FILMS
ABBA-dabba-dooo!!, ABBA In Australia, ABBA: The Movie, Aplauso, ABBA In Concert, Dick Cavett Meets ABBA, Frida The DVD, Gå På Vattnet Om Du Kan, Gäst Hos Hagge, Hylands Hörna, Made In Sweden For Export, När Stenkakan Slog, Nöjesmaskinen, Raskenstam, Senoras y Senores, Stikkan Om Stikkan, Studio 2-ABBA In Poland, Thank You ABBA, The Best Of ABBA—Musikladen Extra, 300 Millones, Words And Music.

INTERNET
Official ABBA website: www.abbasite.com
ABBA-Intermezzo: www.abba-intermezzo.de
ABBA On TV: http://abbaontv.com
ABBA World: http://www.abba-world.net/
Abba4ever Forum: www.abba4ever.com
ABBA For The Record: http://www.abba4therecord.com/
Rafael & Stefan: http://raffem.com/
Carl Magnus Palm: http://www.carlmagnuspalm.com/

INTERNATIONAL ABBA FAN CLUB
P.O. Box 3079
4700 GB Roosendaal
The Netherlands
http://www.abbafanclub.nl/

PICTURE CREDITS

Kjell Johansson: pages 23, 99, 105
Stig Anderson collection: pages 10, 11, 13, 16, 27, 28, 30, 41, 46, 49, 50, 51, 53, 54, 60, 61, 62, 64, 65, 66, 67, 69, 70, 71, 85, 96, 100, 108, 114, 121, 122, 131, 145, 149, 156, 157, 158, 167, 168, 192, 198, 208, 212
Jean-Marie Potiez collection: pages 6, 7, 8, 9, 10, 14, 15, 17, 20, 22, 24, 25, 28, 29, 31, 34, 37, 38, 39, 40, 42, 43, 44, 50, 52, 54, 56, 58, 59, 61, 63, 68, 69, 70, 72, 73, 74, 77, 78, 79, 81, 84, 85, 86, 88, 91, 92, 93, 101, 106, 114, 116, 118, 119, 123, 129, 130, 135, 144, 146, 149, 160, 162, 164, 165, 172, 173, 176, 184, 185, 198, 201, 206, 210, 212, 213, 216, 217, 218, 220, 221, 222, 224, 225, 226, 227, 228, 229, 233, 235, 240
EMI Svenska: pages 18, 19, 20, 21, 30, 32, 33, 36, 37
Polar Music: pages 2, 4, 56-57 (Ola Lager), 105, 128 (Ola Lager), 142, 144, 145, 147, 151, 152, 153, 156, 157, 158, 159, 167, 181 (Mats Bäcker), 199, 200, 204, 207, 208, 209, 213, 218, 224, 226, 227, 228, 229, 234
Jean Pajot: pages 107, 108, 169, 184, 194, 195, 203, 213, 214, 228
Bill Thomas: pages 72, 102, 126, 127, 166, 174, 186, 190, 191, 192, 193, 194, 195
Thierry Lécuyer: pages 169, 214
Vogue Records: pages 55, 65, 69, 71, 74, 75, 76, 77, 79, 86, 87, 89, 93, 95, 101, 160, 165, 170, 175, 190, 203, 221, 227
Universal Music France: pages 109, 123, 129, 143, 176, 181, 190, 219, 223
Guido Marcon: pages 89, 177
Michael Leckebusch: pages 100, 112, 113
Philippe Elan collection: pages 22, 26, 38, 49, 84, 88, 104, 110, 112, 116, 121, 130, 161, 164, 176, 220
RCA: pages 116, 117, 140, 141, 154, 155
Bernd Scheiber collection: pages 118, 221
Claes Setterdahl: pages 200, 202, 206
Jean-Michel Poncelet: page 94
Charlie Bates: page 219
Thomas Engberg: pages 34, 42, 47, 52, 80, 84, 85, 98, 124, 125, 181, 202, 204, 208, 222, 233
Mike Behr: pages 192, 193, 195
Catherine Hinard: page 231
Anderson Records: pages 234, 235 (Carl Bengtsson/Kent Nyberg)
Mono Music: pages 232, 233
WEA: pages 230, 231 (Alberto Tolot)
Dieter Krantz: pages 76, 79, 81, 103, 133, 136, 137, 138, 139, 163
Harry Dean: pages 178, 179
Mayer Mizrahi: page 170
CBS Cupol: pages 106, 107, 187
SVT: pages 48, 96, 97, 122, 123, 206, 207
Rune Söderqvist collection: pages 90, 182, 204, 205
Discomate: pages 171, 196, 197, 198

Costumes sketches by Nora: pages 24, 59, 78

Every reasonable effort has been made to trace the copyright holders of the photographs in this book, but some were unreachable. Any photographer who has not been contacted is invited to write to the publishers in order that full acknowledgement can be made in future editions.

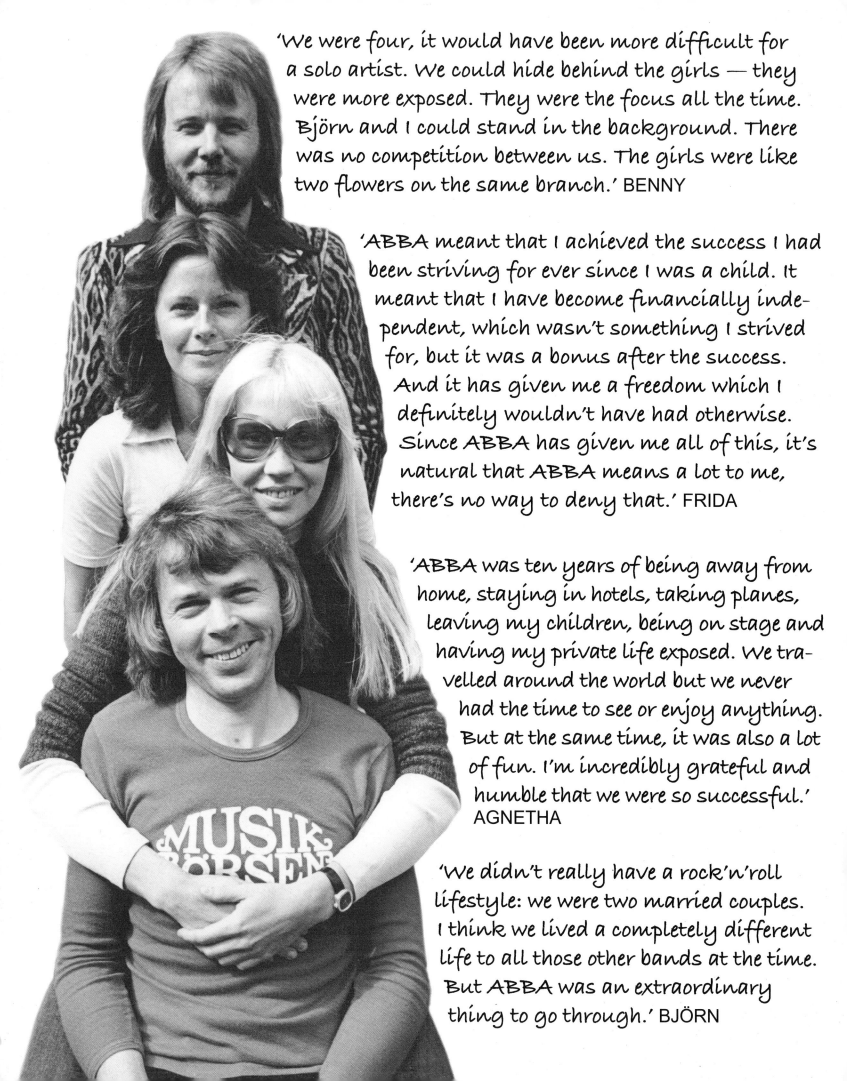

'We were four, it would have been more difficult for a solo artist. We could hide behind the girls — they were more exposed. They were the focus all the time. Björn and I could stand in the background. There was no competition between us. The girls were like two flowers on the same branch.' BENNY

'ABBA meant that I achieved the success I had been striving for ever since I was a child. It meant that I have become financially independent, which wasn't something I strived for, but it was a bonus after the success. And it has given me a freedom which I definitely wouldn't have had otherwise. Since ABBA has given me all of this, it's natural that ABBA means a lot to me, there's no way to deny that.' FRIDA

'ABBA was ten years of being away from home, staying in hotels, taking planes, leaving my children, being on stage and having my private life exposed. We travelled around the world but we never had the time to see or enjoy anything. But at the same time, it was also a lot of fun. I'm incredibly grateful and humble that we were so successful.' AGNETHA

'We didn't really have a rock'n'roll lifestyle: we were two married couples. I think we lived a completely different life to all those other bands at the time. But ABBA was an extraordinary thing to go through.' BJÖRN